Judaism and Vegetarianism

Richard H. Schwartz, Ph.D.

Address inquiries to Micah Publications, 255 Humphrey St., Marblehead, MA 01945.

Quotations from *The Holy Scriptures* are used through the courtesy of The Jewish Publication Society of America.

2nd edition
Printed in the United State of America

Library of Congress CIP

Schwartz, Richard H.
Judaism and vegetarianism

Bibliography: p.
Includes index.
1. Vegetarianism--Religious aspects--Judaism.
2. Ethics, Jewish. I. Title.
BM538.V43S38 1988 296.3'85 88-13525
ISBN 0-916288-30-7
ISBN 0-916288-28-5 (pbk.)

Other books by Richard H. Schwartz, Ph.D.

Judaism and Global Survival, Vantage Press, 1984; Atara Press, 1987.

Mathematics and Global Survival, American Liberty Publishing Co., 1988.

Contents

Foreword

There was a time when Mennaseh reigned in the ancient kingdom of Judah, when the Torah was forgotten in its entirety, and when the people worshipped Baal. Then an ancient scroll of the Law was discovered in the neglected Temple. During the many centuries that followed, parts of the Torah have always been sadly neglected or forgotten, although the writings remained intact.

The practice of vegetarianism is implicit in the teachings of Judaism and is evident from the oft-repeated phrase in Genesis "to man and all creatures wherein there is a living soul." This indicates a common life and a shared destiny and the principle is exemplified throughout biblical writings. Nowhere is it stated that abundance of flesh shall be the reward for observing the Law; rather, there are promises of fruits of the vine and pomegranates, wheat, barley and oil, and peace, when each man shall sit under the shade of his own fig tree, not, let it be noted, under the shadow of his own slaughterhouse.

In recent centuries the section of the Torah that has been almost completely ignored or forgotten is ***tsa'ar ba'alei chayim*** (the mandate to avoid cruelty to animals). True, it is still recited and often some form of observance is retained, but it is an empty husk, a pallid interpretation of a beautiful script. It is like a great actor strutting on the stage of time who has forgotten the part he was intended to play.

Recently the cataclysm of two world wars and the progress of science has metamorphasized people's minds. They now conduct a global war against Creation while giving lip service to spiritual beliefs. They use the latest developments in technology to subjugate their fellow creatures in support of the meat industry. They suppress emotions, sensitivity, and basic rights to domestic animals and reduce their status to the level of commercial, inanimate merchandiseNevertheless, on the horizon, a faint light appears, and slowly public opinion is awakening to the enormity of the crime being committed. The Jewish people, bearing the yoke of the Law, should be in the forefront of a worldwide campaign to halt, at least, the cruelty of the factory farms.

With this growing awareness, the time is most opportune for the appearance of this volume, and Professor Schwartz, by reason of his training and past work, patience, energy, and idealism, is eminently suited to be its author. He has taken every possible opportunity for consultation and explored every avenue for research. The result is a classic work of reference that will assist and guide all those who love Judaism and indeed all seekers after truth, so that they may follow in the footsteps of the many Orthodox Jewish leaders (including several chief rabbis) by discontinuing the obsolete practice of flesh eating. Because almost all of this flesh is produced in the factory farms by unbelievably cruel methods and because these creatures are riddled with antibiotics and sex-change hormones while alive, kashrut can only be truly observed by abstaining therefrom.

May the efforts of the author be blessed with success and may this book be proudly borne aloft on eagles' wings to the far corners of the earth. The author will be rewarded with the knowledge that by his efforts he will bring a step nearer the biblical prophecy that "Israel shall become a blessing unto the nations."

Philip L. Pick
Honorary Life President
Jewish Vegetarian Society
Editor, *The Jewish Vegetarian*

Preface

Judaism and vegetarianism? Can the two be related? After all, what is a *simcha* (Jewish celebration) or holiday dinner without gefilte fish, chopped liver, *cholent*, roast beef, chicken, and chicken soup? And what about passages in the Torah referring to Temple sacrifices of animals and the consumption of meat?

Because of these factors, this book is the result of a leap of faith, an intuition that a religion that has such powerful teachings about compassion for animals, preserving health, feeding the hungry, helping the poor, and conserving resources must be consistent with vegetarianism. As I probed for appropriate Jewish teachings and concepts, I became increasingly convinced that to be more completely involved with the glorious goals and values of Judaism, one should be a vegetarian.

While Judaism emphasizes *tsa'ar ba'alei chayim*, compassion for animals, animals are raised for food today under cruel conditions, in crowded, confined cells, where they are denied fresh air, exercise, and any emotional stimulation.

While Judaism mandates that we be very careful about preserving our health and our lives, flesh-centered diets have been linked to heart disease, several forms of cancer, and other illnesses.

While Judaism stresses that we are to share our bread with the hungry, over 80 percent of grains grown in the United States and other developed countries is fed to animals destined for slaughter, as millions die annually because of hunger and its effects.

While Judaism teaches that "the earth is the Lord's" and we are partners with God in preserving the world and seeing that the earth's resources are properly used, a flesh-centered diet requires the wasteful use of food and other resources, and results in much pollution.

While Judaism stresses that we must seek and pursue peace and that violence results from unjust conditions, flesh-centered diets, by wasting valuable resources, help to perpetuate the widespread hunger and poverty that eventually lead to instability and war.

There are many indications in the Jewish tradition that point toward vegetarianism. The first dietary law (Gen. 1:29) allowed only vegetarian foods. When permission to eat meat was given, as a concession to people's weakness, many prohibitions and restrictions were applied to keep alive a sense of reverence for life. After the Exodus of the Children of Israel from Egypt, a second nonflesh diet was attempted in the form of manna. When the Israelites cried out for meat, God was angry. He finally relented and provided meat, but a plague broke out and many Jews died. According to Rabbi Abraham Kook, the first chief rabbi of the prestate of Israel, based on the prophecy of Isaiah ("...the lion will eat straw like the ox..."), people will again be vegetarians in the time of the Messiah.

Many difficult questions are asked of vegetarians who take the Jewish tradition seriously. These include: Don't we have to eat meat on the Sabbath and to celebrate joyous events? Isn't it a sin not to take advantage of pleasurable things like eating meat? Weren't we given dominion over animals? What about sacrificial Temple services? These and other questions are considered. The 17 questions in the first edition have been increased to 37 in this edition.

A chapter on nutrition has been contributed by Shoshana Margolin, N.D., H.M.D., to ease the way into the world of healthful vegetarian eating. A chapter by Roberta Kalechofsky puts many vegetarian issues into focus.

There have been several recent examples of increased Jewish interest and involvement in vegetarianism. Jewish vegetarian groups and activities in the United States, Britain (where the Jewish Vegetarian Society has its headquarters), and Israel will be discussed. Also, biographies of famous Jewish vegetarians such as Shlomo Goren, the previous Ashkenazi chief rabbi of Israel, Franz Kafka, Isaac Bashevis Singer, and I. L. Peretz will be presented. Finally, an annotated bibliography with many relevant sources is included for those who wish more information on such issues as vegetarianism, nutrition, recipes, and ideas relating Judaism and vegetarianism.

Judaism has much to say about solutions to the critical problems that face the world today. This book is an attempt to show how vegetarianism is consistent with Jewish ideals and can play a role in reducing global problems such as hunger, pollution, resource depletion, poverty, and violence.

This book is only a beginning of the study of an issue that must be considered in depth by the Jewish community.

And God said: "Behold, I have given you every herb yielding seed which is upon the face of all the earth, and every tree, in which is the fruit of a tree yielding seed—to you it shall be for food."

(Genesis 1:29)

RABBINIC ENDORSEMENT

Translated from the Hebrew by Atara Perlman

Congratulations to my friend, Prof. Richard Schwartz; may G-d bless him, for he has worked hard and composed a wonderful work which describes the ideal of vegetarianism and peace of the prophets and sages of Israel as an absolute ideal toward which the laws of our codes and kashrut lead. We look at the vegetarian way of life as a special path of separation and as a step forward toward the "Big Day," i.e., the coming of the Messiah, a day where "Nation shall not lift up sword against nation, neither shall they learn war anymore." (Isaiah 2:4) Bloodshed will cease, and a "Sucking child shall play on the hole of the asp and the weaned child shall put his hand on the basilisk's den." (Isaiah 11:8)

During the Messianic era, when "The lion shall eat straw like the ox," (Isaiah 11:7) man will certainly return to his first stage, before the eating of meat was sanctioned and the consumption of fruits and vegetables will be sufficient. Then there will be total, complete peace between man, his fellowmen, and the animal kingdom. "And the calf and the young lion and the fatling together; And a little child shall lead them." (Isaiah 11:6) Israel and the rest of the world will be blessed, as our Rabbis observed, "Peace was the source of blessings which the Almighty gave to Israel."

Great scholars of Israel, namely the late Chief Rabbi, Harav Abraham Isaac HaCohen Kook, and his outstanding disciple, my own great father, Harav David Cohen, both of blessed memory, expounded admirably in their writings how the laws of the Bible and Talmud mesh with the ideal of peace between man, his fellowmen, and the animal kingdom. This is the desired objective for which we pray and hope.

May it be the will of the Almighty that the number of noble souls will increase amongst our midst, who will be able to observe the dictum of our Rabbis, "Sanctify yourself with that which is permitted unto you"; may they abstain from eating the flesh of living animals and may they be satisfied with the blessings which G-d provided the earth; "And the work of righteousness shall be peace." (Isaiah 32:17) May the knowledge be increased and may the words of the prophet Malachi be realized: "Behold, I will send you Elijah the Prophet before the coming of the great and terrible day of the Lord. And he shall turn the heart of the fathers to their children and the children to their fathers." (Malachi 3:24)

Rabbi Shaar Yashuv Cohen
Chief Rabbi and Rosh Bet Din, Haifa

Acknowledgments

Many thanks are due to Mr. Jonathan Wolf, whose course, Judaism and Vegetarianism, at Lincoln Square Synagogue provided the impetus for this work. Several sections of this book reflect his ideas and those of his students with whom I have had the pleasure of studying. His thorough review of much of the final draft of this edition was extremely valuable.

A prime source of ideas and inspiration has been The Jewish Vegetarian, the magazine of the Jewish Vegetarian Society, edited by Mr. Philip Pick, the honorary president. Without the existence of this group and its quarterly publication, this project would never have started.

In seeking a wide variety of opinions and sources of information, a first draft of this book was written and circulated for comments to people with a wide variety of backgrounds and interests. I express sincere thanks to all who reviewed the first draft and made valuable suggestions, especially the following: Leon Beer, Aviva Cantor, Rabbi Alfred Cohen, Irving Davidson, Jeanne Deutsch, Rabbi Chaim Feuerman, Emilio Fischman, Rabbi Stanley Fogel, Martin Garfinkle, Rabbi Everett Gendler, Dudley Giehl, Sally Gladstein, Rabbi Yaakov Goldberg, Hyman Goldkrantz, Robert Greenberg, Teddy Gross, Joseph Harris, Rabbi Fischel Hochbaum, Roberta Kalechofsky, Mel Kimmel, Zvi Kornblum, Deborah Korngold, Dr. Fred Krause, Rabbi David Lazar, Rabbi Joseph Lazarus, Celia Lubianker, Yvette Mandel, Rabbi Jay Marcus, Dr. Shoshana Margolin, Arlene McCarthy, Philip Pick, Murray Polner, Prof. Margery Robinson, Rabbi H. Rose, Stanley Rubens, Rabbi Murray Schaum, and Rabbi Gerry Serotta.

Among the many people who made valuable comments that helped produce this second edition are: Nathaniel Altman, Susan Asonovic, Philip Becker, Robert Blustein, Mark Mathew Braunstein, Debra Friedman, Rabbi Yonassan Gershom, Rabbi Elyse Goldstein, John Grauer, Robert Greenberg, Rabbi Yaacov Hamnick, Roberta Kalechofsky, Melvin Kimmel, Dr. Michael Klapper, Jay Lavine, M.D., Rabbi David Lazar, Elazer Lew, Rabbi Jay Marcus, Moshe Parry, Murray Polner, Rabbi Abe Raich, Professor Margery Robinson, Joan Rosebury, Steve Rosen, Samuel Schaffe, Sam Schuster, Donald Seeman, Rabbi Robert Seigel, Ellen Sue Spivack, Charles Stahler, Tamir, Rabbi Noach Valley, Jonathan Wolf, and Debra Wasserman.

Special thanks to Dr. Shoshana Margolin, who is sharing with us some of her well-researched and clinically successful approaches to guiding people into a vegetarian life-style, based on scientific nutrition.

Roberta Kalechofsky, head of Micah Press which published this book, made many important suggestions and provided valuable guidance through all phases of the production of this book. She also contributed a chapter which succinctly summarizes the Jewish vegetarian case.

Deep appreciation is expressed to George Platt who took the cover and author's photographs for the first edition with good humor, patience, and professionalism.

Many thanks are due to Lorraine Priester whose great skill with a word processor was invaluable in getting the final manuscript into shape. Also I am grateful to William Portilla of the College of Staten Island's Computer Service Department for his valuable technical advice, to Michael Metz for his expert assistance in typesetting, and to the reprographics staff at the College, especially Gene Rasmussen and Charles Zwirba, for their help in running off the various drafts of the manuscript.

I wish to express deep appreciation to my wife, Loretta, and our children, Susan, David, and Deborah, for their patience, understanding, and encouragement as I used free time from other responsibilities to gather and write this material. They made valuable suggestions on many aspects of this book.

Although all of these above people have been very helpful, the author takes full responsibility for the final selection of material and interpretations.

Finally, I wish to thank in advance all who will read this volume and send me ideas and suggestions for improvements so that this book can better help lead toward that day when "none shall hurt nor destroy in all My holy mountain."

In loving memory of
Bessie and Edward Susskind
whose guidance and devotion were always an inspiration

1

A Vegetarian View of the Bible

> And God said: "Behold, I have given you every herb yielding seed which is upon the face of all the earth, and every tree, in which is the fruit of a tree yielding seed—to you it shall be for food." (Gen. 1:29)

God's initial intention was that people should be vegetarians.

The famous Jewish Torah commentator, Rashi (1040-1105), states the following about God's first dietary law:

> God did not permit Adam and his wife to kill a creature and to eat it flesh. Only every green herb shall they all eat together.[1]

Many other Torah commentators agree with this assessment, including Abraham Ibn Ezra (1092-1167), Maimonides (1135-1214), Nachmanides (1194-1270), and Rabbi Joseph Albo (died in 1444). Later scholars such as Rabbi Samson Raphael Hirsch (1808-1888), Moses Cassuto (1883-1951), and Nechama Leibowitz (born 1905), concur. Cassuto, for example, in his commentary *From Adam to Noah* (p. 58) states:

> You are permitted to use the animals and employ them for work, have dominion over them in order to utilize their services for your subsistence, but must not hold their life cheap nor slaughter them for food. Your natural diet is vegetarian...[2]

The Talmud agrees that people were initially vegetarians: "Adam was not permitted meat for purposes of eating."[3]

The great 13th century Jewish philosopher Nachmanides states that this initial dietary law was

> because living creatures possess a moving soul and a certain spiritual superiority which in this respect make them similar to those who possess intellect (people) and they have the power of affecting their welfare and their food and they flee from pain and death.[4]

According to the Jewish philosopher Joseph Albo, the reason is that "In the killing of animals there is cruelty, rage, and the accustoming of oneself to the bad habit of shedding innocent blood..."[5]

God's first dietary law is a unique statement in humanity's spiritual history. It is a spiritual blueprint of a vegetarian world order. Yet how many millions of people have read this Torah verse and passed it by without considering its meaning?

After stating that people were to adhere to a vegetarian diet, the Torah next indicates that animals were not to prey on one another but were also to have only vegetarian food:

> And to every beast of the earth, and to every fowl of the air, and to every thing that creepeth upon the earth, wherein there is a living soul, [I have given] every green herb for food. (Gen. 1:30)

Immediately after giving these dietary laws, God saw everything that he had made and "behold, it was very good" (Gen. 1:31). Everything in the universe was as God wanted it, with nothing superfluous and nothing lacking, a complete harmony.[6] The vegetarian diet was consistent with God's initial plan.

There are other indications in early chapters of Genesis that people originally were to be sustained on vegetarian diets:

> And the Lord God commanded the man, saying: "of every tree of the garden, thou mayest freely eat..." (Gen. 2:16)

> ...and thou shalt eat the herbs of the field. (Gen. 3:18)

Chapter 5 of Genesis tells of the long lives of people in the generations of the vegetarian period from Adam to Noah. Adam lived 930 years; Seth (Adam's son) lived 912 years; Enosh (Seth's son) lived 905 years; Kenan (Enosh's son) lived 910 years; and so on, until Methuselah, who lived 969 years, the longest time of life recorded in the Torah. After the flood, people lived for much shorter periods. Abraham, for example, lived only 175 years.

Why the tremendous change in life spans? Before the flood, people were forbidden to eat meat; after the flood it was permitted (Gen. 9:3). A partial explanation, therefore, may be that it was the change in diet that contributed to the change in life spans. This view was held by the Jewish philosopher and Bible commentator Nachmanides.[7] Recent evidence linking heavy meat consumption with several diseases reinforces this point of view (see chapter 3). Of course, a shift to sensible vegetarian diets will not increase life spans to anywhere near those of early people, but recent medical evidence indicates that it *would* lead to an increase in the average span and quality of life.

The strongest support for vegetarianism as a positive ideal anywhere in Torah literature is in the writing of Rabbi Abraham Isaac Hacohen Kook (1865-1935). Rav Kook was the first Chief Rabbi of pre-state Israel and a highly respected and beloved Jewish spiritual leader in the early 20th century. He was a mystical thinker, a forceful writer, and a great Torah scholar. His powerful words on vegetarianism are found primarily in *A Vision of Vegetarianism and Peace* (edited by Rabbi David Cohen, "The Nazir").

Rav Kook believes that the permission to eat meat was only a temporary concession; he feels that a God who is merciful to his creatures would not institute an everlasting law permitting the killing of animals for food.[8] He states:

> It is inconceivable that the Creator who had planned a world of harmony and a perfect way for man to live should, many thousands of years later, find that this plan was wrong.[9]

People are not always ready to live up to God's highest ideals. By the time of Noah, humanity had degenerated greatly. "And God saw the earth, and behold it was corrupt; for all flesh had corrupted their way upon the earth" (Gen. 6:12). People had sunk so low that they would eat a limb torn from a living animal. As a concession to people's weakness,[10] permission to eat meat was then given:

> Every moving thing that lives shall be food for you; as the green herb have I given you all. (Gen. 9:3)

Joseph Albo states that God's commandments were designed to inculcate in people a higher level of spirituality; but in dealing with people as they were, not as they should be, God permitted the eating of meat.[11] Evidently people's appetite for flesh was such that God felt it better to permit the eating of meat and regulate it, rather than to have people harbor a forbidden appetite, which before the flood had lead to corruption.

According to Rav Kook, because people had sunk to an extremely low level of spirituality, it was necessary that they be given an elevated image of themselves as compared to animals, and that they concentrate their efforts into first improving relationships between people. He feels that were people denied the right to eat meat, they might eat the flesh of human beings due to their inability to control their lust for flesh. He regards the permission to slaughter animals for food as a "transitional tax" or temporary dispensation until a "brighter era" is reached when people would return to vegetarian diets.[12]

Isaak Hebenstreit was a Polish rabbi who wrote *Kivrot Hata'avah* (the graves of lust) in 1929. He stated that God never wanted people to eat meat, because of the cruelty involved; people shouldn't kill any living thing and fill their stomachs by destroying others. He believed that God temporarily gave permission to eat meat because of the conditions after the flood, when all plant life had been destroyed.[13]

Just prior to granting Noah and his family permission to eat meat, God stated:

> And the fear of you and the dread of you shall be upon every beast of the earth, and upon every fowl of the air, and upon all wherewith the ground teemeth, and upon all the fishes of the sea: into your hand are they delivered. (Gen. 9:2)

Now that there is permission to eat animals, no longer do people and animals work together in harmony, but living creatures fear and dread human beings. Rabbi Samson Raphael Hirsch, a famous nineteenth-century Torah commentator, stated that the attachment between people and animals was broken which initiated a change in the relationship of people to the world.[14]

The permission given to Noah to eat meat was not unconditional. There was an immediate prohibition against eating blood:

> "Only flesh with the life thereof, which is the blood thereof, shall ye not eat." (Gen. 9:4)

Similar statements are made in Leviticus 19:26, 17:10,12 and Deuteronomy 12:16,23,25, and 15:23. The Torah identifies blood with life: "...for the blood is the life" (Deut. 12:23). Life must already have departed from the animal before it can be eaten.

A modern rabbi, Samuel Dresner, commenting on the dietary laws indicates:

> The removal of blood which kashrut teaches is one of the most powerful means of making us constantly aware of the concession and compromise which the whole act of eating meat, in reality, is. Again it teaches us reverence for life.[15]

Biblical commentator Moses Cassuto states:

> Apparently the Torah was in principle opposed to the eating of meat. When Noah and his descendants were permitted to eat meat this was a concession conditional on the prohibition of the blood. This prohibition implied respect for the principle of life ("for the blood is the life") and an allusion to the fact that in reality all meat should have been prohibited. This partial prohibition was designed to call to mind the previously total one.[16]

Immediately after permission was given to eat meat, God stated, "And surely, your blood of your lives will I require" (Gen. 9:5). The rabbis base the prohibition of suicide on these words.[17] But coming directly after flesh is allowed, a vegetarian might reason, this passage hints that eating meat is a slow form of suicide. Perhaps God is warning us: "I prefer that you do not eat meat. But, if you must eat meat, there will be a penalty—your life blood will I require."[18] That is, your life will be shortened by eating something that you were not meant to eat. In other words, if people choose to live in violence, by slaughtering and eating animals, they must pay the necessary penalty. Note that this speculation is consistent with the decrease in life spans that occurred after permission to eat meat was given and also with modern research in health and nutrition.

According to Isaac Arama (1420-1494), author of *Akedat Yitzhak*, and others, after the Israelites left Egypt, God tried to establish another non-meat diet, manna.[19] Manna is described in the Torah as a vegetarian food, "like coriander seed" (Num. 11:7). The rabbis of the Talmud stated that the manna had whatever taste and flavor the eater desired at the time of eating. It must also have had sufficient nutrient value because Moses stated that "It is the bread which the Lord hath given you to eat" (Exod. 16:15).

Rabbi J. H. Hertz commented on the manna: "God in His ever-sustaining providence fed Israel's host during the weary years of wandering in His own unsearchable way."[20]

The manna taught the Children of Israel several lessons, which are interesting from a vegetarian point of view.

(1) God provides for our needs; manna was available for each day's requirements.

In the same way, vegetarian diets could result in enough food for all. A meat diet leads to scarcity of food for some and the potential for violence (see chapters 4 and 6).

(2) We should be content with what we have.[21] Each person was to gather one omer (a measure of manna), but some gathered more and some less. When they measured it out, they found that whether they had gathered much or little, they had just enough to meet their needs.

Again, a vegetarian diet would provide enough for everyone's needs. With a meat-centered diet, the few eat more than they need, and many millions are malnourished.

(3) Enough was provided on Friday morning so that there was no need to gather manna on the Sabbath. The people were commanded to rest on the seventh day.

With a vegetarian diet, people would not need to struggle continually for their means of subsistence. They would be able truly to rest, to have a peaceful Sabbath, knowing that their needs would be met and that there is no reason to struggle for necessities.

The people were not satisfied, however, with the simple diet of manna, which sustained them in the desert. The mixed multitude that was with the Jewish people lusted for meat, and the Children of Israel complained, "Would that we were given flesh to eat." They said they remembered the fish and other good food that they believed they had had in Egypt, but now they had only manna to eat. The Lord was very angry and Moses was displeased. Finally, God provided meat in the form of quails, which were brought by a wind from the sea. While the flesh was in their mouths, before it was chewed, the anger of God was kindled against the people; He struck them with a great plague (Num. 11:4-33).

Note the following key points from a vegetarian point of view: (1) God wanted the people to be sustained on manna; He was greatly angry when they cried for flesh to eat. (2) God did provide meat, but a plague broke out among the people. Perhaps this incident was designed to teach people that they should not eat meat, and if they did, it would have very negative consequences. (3) The place where this incident occurred was named "The Graves of Lust," to indicate that the lust for flesh led to the many deaths (Num. 11:34). While the manna, their staple food in the desert, kept them in good health for forty years, many deaths occurred when they deviated from this simple diet.

When the Israelites were in the wilderness, animals could only be slaughtered and eaten as part of the sacrificial service in the sanctuary (Lev. 17:3-5). Maimonides states that the sacrifices were a concession to the primitive practices of the nations at that time.[22] This will be discussed in more detail in chapter 7, Question 5.

Finally God permitted people to eat meat even if it wasn't part of a sacrificial offering:

> When the Lord thy God shall enlarge thy border as He hath promised thee, and thou shalt say: "I will eat flesh," because thy soul desireth to eat flesh; thou mayest eat flesh, after all the desire of thy soul. (Deut. 12:20)

This permitted meat was called *b'sar ta'avah*, "meat of lust," so named because meat is not considered a necessity for life.[23]

The above verse does not command that people eat meat. Rabbinic tradition perceives it to indicate that it is people's desire to eat flesh and not God's edict that people do so. Even while arguing against vegetarianism as a moral cause, Rabbi Elijah Judah Schochet, author of *Animal Life in Jewish Tradition*, (1984), concedes that "Scripture does not command the Israelite to eat meat, but rather permits this diet as a concession to lust."[24] Similarly, another critic of vegetarian activism, Rabbi J. David Bleich, a noted modern Torah scholar and professor at Yeshiva University, concedes, "the implication is that meat may be consumed when there is desire and appetite for it as food, but may be eschewed when there is not desire and, *a fortiori*, when it is found to be repugnant."[25] In short, again according to Rabbi Bleich, "Jewish tradition does not command carnivorous behavior..."[26]

Rabbi I. Hebenstreit pointed out that God did not want to give the Israelites who had left Egypt permission to return to a diet involving meat, due to the cruelty involved. However, the mixed-multitude (other slaves who left Egypt with the Jews) lusted for meat and inculcated this desire among the Jewish people. Hence God again reluctantly gave permission for the consumption of meat, but with many restrictions.[27]

The negative connotation associated with the consumption of meat is indicated in the Talmud:

> The Torah teaches a lesson in moral conduct, that man shall not eat meat unless he has a special craving for it...and shall eat it only occasionally and sparingly.[28]

The sages also felt that eating meat was not for everyone:

> Only a scholar of Torah may eat meat, but one who is ignorant of Torah is forbidden to eat meat.[29]

Based on this prohibition, how many Jews today can consider themselves so scholarly as to be able to eat meat? And those who do diligently study the Torah and are aware of conditions related to the production and consumption of meat today would, I believe, come to conclusions similar to those in this book.

It should be noted that the above stricture reflected concern for the scrupulous observance of the many technicalities of the laws of kashrut. While there are few conditions on the consumption of vegetarian foods, only a diligent Torah scholar can fathom the myriad regulations governing the eating of meat.

Rabbi Kook believes that the permission to eat meat "after all the desire of your soul" was a concealed reproach and a qualified command.[30] He states that a day will come when people will detest the eating of the flesh of animals because of a moral loathing, and then it shall be said that "because your soul does not long to eat meat, you will not eat meat."[31]

The Torah looks favorably on vegetarian foods. Flesh foods are often mentioned with distaste and are associated with lust (lack of control over one's appetite for meat). In the Song of Songs, the divine bounty is mentioned in terms of fruits, vegetables, vines, and nuts. There is no special b'racha (blessing) recited before eating meat or fish, as there is for other foods such as bread, cake, wine, fruits, and vegetables; the blessing for meat is a general one, the same as that over water or any other undifferentiated food.

Rabbi Yonassan Gershom, a modern chassidic rebbe from Minnesota, states that "concerning the priority given to blessings, meat is on the bottom of the hierarchy". He notes that on festivals and sabbaths, wine comes first. Otherwise bread comes first, and a blessing over bread covers *all* other foods except wine. If there is no bread, foods are blessed in the following order: (1) wine, (2) grains, (3) tree fruits, (4) vegetables, (5) all other foods, including fish, meats, etc. In other words, meat has the lowest priority in the *b'racha* system. Also, when bread is eaten a full *bircat hamazon* (blessing after meals) is to be recited. For the grains and fruits mentioned in the Torah (the seven species), there is a shorter blessing recited after meals (*al hamichya*), but if only other foods such as meat or fish are eaten, only one sentence is to be recited afterwards (*borei nefashot*). Since, as our sages taught, words have replaced sacrifices today, flesh foods are least honored.

Typical of the Torah's emphasis on nonflesh foods are the following:

> For the Lord thy God bringeth thee into a good land, a land of brooks of water, of fountains and depths, springing forth in valleys and hills; a land of wheat and barley, of vines and fig-trees and pomegranates; a land of olive-trees and honey; a land wherein thou shalt eat bread without scarceness, thou shalt not lack anything in it...And thou shalt eat and be satisfied, and bless the Lord thy God for the good land which He hath given thee. (Deut. 8:7-10)

> I will give you the rain of your land in its due season, the first rain and the latter rain, that thou may gather in thy corn, and thy wine, and thy oil. (Deut. 11:14)

Among many similar statements by the prophets are:

> I shall return my people from captivity, and they shall build up the waste cities and inhabit them, and they shall plant vineyards and drink the wine from them, and they shall make gardens and eat the fruit from them, and I shall plant them upon their land. (Amos 9:14-15)

> Build ye houses and dwell in them, and plant gardens and eat the fruit of them. (Jeremiah 29:5)

Along with permission to eat meat, many laws and restrictions (the laws of kashrut) were given. Rabbi Kook believes that the reprimand implied by these regulations is an elaborate apparatus designed to keep alive a sense of reverence for life, with the aim of eventually leading people away from their meat-eating habit.[32]

This idea is echoed by Torah commentator Solomon Efraim Lunchitz, author of *K'lee Yakar*:

> What was the necessity for the entire procedure of ritual slaughter? For the sake of self-discipline. It is far more appropriate for man not to eat meat; only if he has a strong desire for meat does the Torah permit it, and even this only after the trouble and inconvenience necessary to satisfy his desire. Perhaps because of the bother and annoyance of the whole procedure, he will be restrained from such a strong and uncontrollable desire for meat.[33]

A similar statement is made by a modern rabbi, Pinchas Peli:

> Accordingly, the laws of kashrut come to teach us that a Jew's first preference should be a vegetarian meal. If however one cannot control a craving for meat, it should be kosher meat, which would serve as a reminder that the animal being eaten is a creature of God, that the death of such a creature cannot be taken lightly, that hunting for sport is forbidden, that we cannot treat any living thing callously, and that we are responsible for what happens to other beings (human or animal) even if we did not personally come into contact with them.[34]

Rav Kook sees people's craving for meat as a manifestation of negative passions rather than an inherent need. He and Joseph Albo believe that in the days of the Messiah people will again be vegetarians.[35] Rav Kook states that in the Messianic Epoch, "the effect of knowledge will spread even to animals...and sacrifices in the Temple will consist of vegetation, and it will be pleasing to God as in days of old..."[36] They base this on the prophecy of Isaiah:

> *And the wolf shall dwell with the lamb,*
> *And the leopard shall lie down with the kid;*
> *And the calf and the young lion and the fatling together;*
> *And a little child shall lead them*
> *And the cow and the bear shall feed;*

Their young ones shall lie down together,
And the lion shall eat straw like the ox....
They shall not hurt nor destroy in all My holy mountain.
(Isa. 11:6-9)

Rabbi Kook believes that the high moral level involved in the vegetarianism of the generations before Noah, is a virtue of such great value that it cannot be lost forever.[37] In the future ideal state, just as at the initial period, people and animals will not eat flesh.[38] No one shall hurt or destroy another living creature. People's lives will not be supported at the expense of the lives of animals.

Other prophetic visions that depict vegetarian diets for people include:

> And it shall come to pass in that day that mountains shall drip sweet wine and the hills shall flow with milk. (Joel 4:18)

> And they shall plant vineyards and drink the wine thereof; they shall also make gardens and eat the fruit of them. (Amos 9:14)

> And the earth shall respond to the corn, the wine, and the oil. (Hosea 2:24)

In his booklet which summarizes many of Rav Kook's teachings, Joe Green, a recent Jewish vegetarian writer, concluded that Jewish religious ethical vegetarians are pioneers of the Messianic era; they are leading lives that make the coming of the Messiah more likely.[39]

Today most Jews eat meat, but the high ideal of God, the initial vegetarian dietary law, still stands supreme in the Bible for Jews and the whole world to see, an ultimate goal toward which all people should strive.

2

Tsa'ar Ba'alei Chayim - Judaism and Compassion for Animals

> While our teacher Moses was tending the sheep of Jethro in the wilderness a kid ran away from him. He ran after it until it reached Hasuah. Upon reaching Hasuah it came upon a pool of water [whereupon] the kid stopped to drink. When Moses reached it he said, "I did not know that you were running because [you were] thirsty. You must be tired." He placed it on his shoulder and began to walk. The Holy One, blessed be He, said, "You are compassionate in leading flocks belonging to mortals; I swear you will similarly shepherd my flock, Israel."
>
> Exodus Rabbah 2:2

Animals are part of God's creation and people have special responsibilities to them. The Jewish tradition clearly indicates that we are forbidden to be cruel to animals and that we are to treat them with compassion. These concepts are summarized in the Hebrew phrase *tsa'ar ba'alei chayim*, the biblical mandate not to cause "pain to any living creature."

Psalms 104 and 148 show God's close identification with the beasts of the field, creatures of the sea, and birds of the air. Sea animals and birds received the same blessing as people: " Be fruitful and multiply" (Gen. 1:22). Animals were initially given a vegetarian diet, similar to that of people (Gen. 1:29-30). The important Hebrew term nefesh chaya (a "living soul") was applied in Genesis (1:21, 1:24) to animals as well as people. Although the Torah clearly indicates that people are to have "dominion over the fish of the sea, and over the fowl of the air, and over every living thing that creepeth upon the earth" (Gen. 1:28), there was to be a basic relatedness, and the rights and privileges of animals were not to be neglected or overlooked. Animals are also God's creatures, possessing sensitivity and the capacity for feeling pain; hence they must be protected and treated with compassion and justice.

God even made treaties and covenants with animals just as with humans:

> "As for me," sayeth the Lord, "behold I establish My Covenant with you and with your seed after you, and with every living creature that is with you, the fowl, the cattle, and every beast of the earth with you; of all that go out of the ark, even every beast of the earth." (Gen. 9:9-10)

> And in that day will I make a covenant for them with the beasts of the field and with the fowls of heaven and with the creeping things of the ground. And I will break the bow and the sword and the battle out of the land and I will make them to lie down safely. (Hos. 2:20)

Ecclesiastes cynically considers the kinship between people and animals. Both are described as sharing the common fate of mortality:

> For that which befalleth the sons of men befalleth beasts;
> even one thing befalleth them;
> as the one dieth, so dieth the other;
> yea, they all have one breath;
> so that man hath no preeminence above a beast;
> for all is vanity.
> All go to one place; all are of the dust.
> who knoweth the spirit of men whether it goeth upward;
> and the spirit of the beast whether it goeth
> downward to the earth?
>
> (Ecclesiastes 3:19-21)

God considered animals, as well as people, when he admonished Jonah,

> and should I not have pity on Nineveh, that great city, wherein are more than sixscore thousand persons...and also much cattle. (Jonah 4:11)

The Psalms indicate God's concern for animals, for "His tender mercies are over all His creatures" (Ps. 145:9). They pictured God as "satisfying the desire of every living creature" (Ps. 145:16), "providing food for the beasts and birds" (Ps. 147:9), and, in general, "preserving both man and beast" (Ps. 36:7).

God is depicted as providing each animal with the attributes necessary for survival in its environment. For example, the camel has a short tail so that its tail won't become ensnared when it feeds upon thorns; the ox has a long tail so that it can protect itself from gnats when it feeds on the plains; the feelers of locusts are flexible so that they won't be blinded by their feelers breaking against trees.[1]

Perhaps the Jewish attitude toward animals is best summarized by the statement in Proverbs 12:10, "The righteous person regards the life of his beast." This is the human counterpoint of "The Lord is good to all, and His tender mercies are over all His creatures" (Ps. 145:9). In Judaism, one who is cruel to animals cannot be regarded as a righteous individual.

TORAH LAWS INVOLVING COMPASSION FOR ANIMALS

(1) It is forbidden to cause pain to any animal.

Maimonides[2] and R. Judah ha-Hasid[3] (1150-1217) state that this is based on the biblical statement of the angel of God to Balaam, "Wherefore hast thou smitten thine ass?" (Num. 22:32). This verse is used in the Talmud as a prime source for its assertion that we are to treat animals humanely.[4]

The *Code of Jewish Law* is more explicit and specific.[5]

> It is forbidden, according to the law of the Torah, to inflict pain upon any living creature. On the contrary, it is our duty to relieve the pain of any creature, even if it is ownerless or belongs to a non-Jew.

> When horses, drawing a cart, come to a rough road or a steep hill, and it is hard for them to draw the cart without help, it is our duty to help them, even when they belong to a non-Jew, because of the precept not to be cruel to animals, lest the owner smite them to force them to draw more than their strength permits.
>
> It is forbidden to tie the legs of a beast or of a bird in a manner as to cause them pain.

(2) "Thou shalt not muzzle the ox when he treadeth out the corn" (Deut. 25:4).

At the time of threshing, when the ox is surrounded by the food that it enjoys so much, it should not be prevented from satisfying its appetite. Rabbi Samson Raphael Hirsch states that this prohibition gives to the animal which helps you to take possession of the fruits of the earth a right to these fruits while it is working; no means may be used to prevent it from eating[6]... He cites the *Shulchan Aruch*[7] as indicating that one may prevent an animal from eating when the fruits might harm it.[8] Rashi, citing Talmud Baba Kamma 54b in support, states that this law also applies to other animals, including birds.[9]

Professor C. H. Cornill contrasted the humanitarianism of this law with the grape harvest where "one of the richest Italian real estate owners fastened iron muzzles to the miserable, fever- stricken workmen, so that it might not occur to these poor peasants working for starvation wages under the glowing sun of Southern Italy, to satiate their burning thirst and their gnawing hunger with a few of the millions of grapes of the owner."[10] Because of this and similar legislation, William Lecky, the distinguished British historian, stated that "tenderness to animals is one of the most beautiful features in the Old Testament."[11]

(3) "Thou shalt not plow with an ox and an ass together" (Deut. 22:10).

Such an act would cause the weaker animal great pain in trying to keep up with the stronger. The stronger would also suffer by being deprived of its usual routine, by having to act contrary to its instinctive nature. The Talmud extends this law to apply to any case where there are two animals involved, one strong and one weak, and to other activities such as driving carts or wagons.[12]

> You may not allow one task to be done together by animals of two species. You may not allow them to carry the smallest thing together, even if it be only a seed.... You may not sit in a wagon drawn by animals of differing species.[13]

Rabbi Hirsch concludes that one should not unite animals for any activities that God's laws have not designed for working together in the service of the world.[14]

(4) "A person should not eat or drink before first providing for his animals."[15]

This is based on Deuteronomy (11:15): "And I will give grass in thy fields for thy cattle, and thou shalt eat and be satisfied." God provides food for the cattle before people and we are to imitate God.

According to R. Eleazer ha-Kapar, a talmudic sage, no one should buy a domestic animal, wild beast, or bird unless he is able to feed it properly.[16] The duty to feed an animal first is so great that a person is legally authorized to interrupt the performance of a rabbinic commandment in order to ascertain that this has been done.[17]

(5) Animals too must be able to rest on the Sabbath day.

The *kiddush* (sanctification over wine or grape juice) that is recited on Sabbath mornings includes the following verse from the Ten Commandments:

> Remember the Sabbath day, to keep it holy. Six days shalt thou labor, and do all thy work; but the seventh day is a sabbath unto the Lord, thy God, in it thou shalt not do any manner of work, thou, nor thy son, nor thy daughter, nor thy man-servant, nor thy maid-servant, nor thy *cattle*, nor thy stranger that is within thy gates.
>
> (Exod. 20:8-10)

Similar statements occur in Exodus 23:12 and Deuteronomy 5:12-14. Based on these Torah statements, Rashi states that animals must be free to roam on the Sabbath day and graze freely and enjoy the beauties of nature.[18] The fact that animals are considered within the Ten Commandments indicates the emphasis placed on compassion for animals in Judaism. Rabbi J. H. Hertz, in commenting on Exodus 20:10, states:

> It is one of the glories of Judaism that, thousands of years before anyone else, it so fully recognized our duties to (animals).[19]

In a similar manner, animals are to be provided for during the Sabbatical year; the produce that grows freely during that period is to be enjoyed by the beasts of the field as well as the poor. (Lev. 25:6-7)

(6) It is forbidden to sacrifice a newborn ox, sheep, or goat until it has had at least seven days of warmth and nourishment from its mother (Lev. 22:27).

This commandment shows the desire of the Torah to spare the feelings of living creatures and to instill a spirit of mercy in people. Then why did God permit the killing of animals at all? Some suggest that it was a concession to people's weakness and to the primitive practices of many nations during the biblical period.

(7) "And whether it be ox or ewe, ye shall not kill it and its young both in one day" (Lev. 22:28).

This forbids a custom, usual in foreign cults, of sacrificing an animal and its young together. Maimonides comments on this verse as follows:

> It is prohibited to kill an animal with its young on the same day, in order that people should be restrained and prevented from killing the two together in such a manner that the young is slain in the sight of the mother; for the pain of animals under such circumstances is very great. There is no difference in this case between the pain of people and the pain of other living beings, since the love and the tenderness of the mother for her young ones is not produced by reasoning but by feeling, and this faculty exists not only in people but in most living things.[20]

(8) We are forbidden to take the mother bird and its young together. The mother bird must be sent away before its young are taken. (Deut. 22:6-7).

For the compassion that we show to the mother bird, we are promised a long life. Maimonides comments that when the mother bird is sent away she does not see the taking of her young ones and does not feel any pain at that time.[21] Furthermore, in most cases, the commandment will result in the entire nest being left untouched, because the young or the eggs, which people are allowed to take, are generally unfit for human food.[22] He also states that if we are commanded not to cause grief to animals and to birds, how much more careful must we be not to cause grief to people.[23]

Some Jewish scholars, including Nachmanides, Bahya b. Asher (died in 1340), and the Kol Bo (late 13th century) connected the above law and others prohibiting slaughter of an animal together with its young to the preservation of species, rather than abhorrence of cruelty toward animals.[24]

(9) We should not boil a kid in the milk of its mother (Exodus 23:19, 34:26; Deuteronomy 14:21).

Commenting on Exodus 23:19, Rashi notes that the repetition of this prohibition in three different biblical passages implies a three-fold ban: milk and meat must not be eaten together; they must not be cooked together; and it is forbidden to benefit from food containing a mixture of milk and meat.

Some Torah commentators saw the above law as a rejection of an ancient pagan practice. Ibn Ezra viewed boiling a kid in its mother's milk as an example of extreme barbarism.[25] The Rashbam (1080-1174) considered the practice as denoting gross insensitivity and cruelty.[26]

(10) Animals should not be allowed to suffer discomfort:

> If thou see the ass of him that hateth thee lying under its burden, thou shalt surely not pass by him; thou shalt surely unload it with him. (Exod. 23:5)

This commandment has both a humane motive toward the animal and a charitable motive toward an enemy. The talmudic rabbis taught that the greatest hero is a person who turns an enemy into a friend.[27] The Talmud states that the obligation to relieve an animal from pain or danger supercedes rabbinic ordinances related to the Sabbath.[28]

(11) We must be vigilant for the well-being of a lost animal:

> Thou shalt not see thy brother's ox or his sheep driven away and hide thyself from them; thou shalt surely bring them back unto thy brother. (Deut. 22:1).

In addition, the animal must be cared for, until the owner's return.

(12) The rabbis strongly disapproved of hunting as a sport.[29]

A Jew is permitted to capture fish, flesh, or fowl only for purposes of human food or another essential human need, but to destroy an animal for "sport" constitutes wanton destruction and is to be condemned. Based on the statement "not to stand in the way of sinners" (Ps. 1:1), the Talmud prohibits association with hunters[30]. A query was addressed to Rabbi Ezekiel Landau (1713-93) by a man wishing to know if he could hunt in his large estate, which included forests and fields. The response stated:

> In the Torah the sport of hunting in imputed only to fierce characters like Nimrod and Esau, never to any of the patriarchs and their descendants.... I cannot comprehend how a Jew could even dream of killing animals merely for the pleasure of hunting.... When the act of killing is prompted by that of sport, it is downright cruelty.[31]

(13) Shechitah (Jewish ritual slaughter).

Because, as indicated previously, the consumption of meat was permitted as a concession to people's weakness and people thought it was necessary for proper nutrition, it was desired to make slaughter as painless as possible through *shechitah* (the laws of ritual slaughter). The laws of *shechitah* provide the most humane way of slaughtering animals.[32] The knife to be used is regularly examined to ensure that it is perfectly smooth, without a notch that might tear the flesh. The arteries to the head of the animal are severed by the cut, thus stopping blood circulation to the head and making the animal oblivious to any pain.

The slaughterer, the *shochet*, must be carefully chosen. He is obligated to examine the animal for any possible disease and to slaughter the animal according to Jewish law. The *shochet* is required to be a pious and learned person. He must prove his complete knowledge of the laws of *shechitah*. He must recite a blessing prior to slaughter as a reminder that he must have reverence for the life that he takes. Thus the laws of *shechitah* teach that meat-eating is a concession to people's weakness. Question 6 in chapter 7 will consider *shechitah* further.

(14) On Yom Kippur, the most sacred day of the Jewish year, when Jews fast and pray for life and good health from God in the coming year, it is forbidden to wear leather shoes. One reason is related to our behavior toward God's creatures; it is not proper to plead for compassion when one has not shown compassion toward other living creatures.[33]

Rabbi Moses Isserles (1525 or 1530-1572), known as the Rema, states: "How can a man put on shoes, a piece of clothing for which it is necessary to kill a living thing, on Yom Kippur, which is a day of grace and compassion, when it is written 'His tender mercies are over all His works' (Ps. 145:9)."[34]

Although Jews are required to recite a special benediction, "Blessed are thou, O Lord our God, King of the Universe, who has kept us in life, and hast preserved us, and has enabled us to reach this season," when putting on a piece of clothing for the first time, an exception is made for furs and leather shoes because an animal had to be killed in making them.[35]

The *Code of Jewish Law*[36] has a similar statement:

> It is customary to say to one who puts on a new garment: "Mayest thou wear it out and acquire a new one." But we do not express this wish to one who puts on new shoes or a new garment made of fur or leather... because a garment like this requires the killing of a living creature, and it is written: "And His mercy is upon all his works" (Ps. 145:9).

(15) Although the Torah contains no explicit rule prohibiting cruelty to animals in general, there are so many commandments mandating humane treatment for them that the rabbis explicitly declared that consideration for animals is a biblical law.[37] Hence, various rabbinic Sabbath laws could be relaxed to show compassion to or avoid harm to an animal. For such purposes, one has permission to capture them,[38] take care of their wounds when they are fresh and painful,[39] race them to exhaustion as a remedy for overeating,[40] place them in water to cool them following an attack of congestion,[41] and raise them from water into which they have fallen.[42]

Rabbi Samson Raphael Hirsch eloquently summarizes the Jewish view on treatment of animals:

> Here you are faced with God's teaching, which obliges you not only to refrain from inflicting unnecessary pain on any animal, but to help and, when you can, to lessen the pain whenever you see an animal suffering, even through no fault of yours.[43]

EXAMPLES OF KINDNESS TO ANIMALS SHOWN BY GREAT JEWISH HEROES

Many great Jewish heroes of the Bible were trained for their tasks by being shepherds of flocks.

As the *midrash* quoted at the beginning of this chapter indicates, Moses was tested by God through his shepherding. The greatest Jewish teacher, leader, and prophet was found worthy, not because of abilities as a speaker, statesman, politician, or warrior, but because of his compassion for animals!

God also deemed David worthy of tending the Jewish people because he, like Moses, knew how to look after sheep, bestowing upon each the care it needed. David used to prevent the larger sheep from going out before the smaller ones. The smaller ones were then able to graze upon the tender grass. Next he permitted the old sheep to feed from the ordinary grass, and finally the young, lusty sheep at the tougher grass.[44]

Rebecca was judged suitable as Isaac's wife because of the kindness she showed to animals. Eliezer, Abraham's servant, asked Rebecca for water for himself. She not only gave him water, but also ran to provide water for his camels. Rebecca's concern for camels was evidence of a tender heart and compassion for all God's creatures. It convinced Eliezer that Rebecca would make a suitable wife for Isaac (Gen. 24:11-20).

The patriarch Jacob also demonstrated concern for animals. After their reconciliation, his brother Esau said to him, "Let us take our journey and let us go, and I will go before thee." But Jacob, concerned about his flocks and children, politely replied: "My lord knoweth that the children are tender, and that the flocks and the herds giving suck are a care to me; and if my workers overdrive them one day, all the flocks will die. Let my lord, I pray thee, pass over before his servant and I will journey on gently, according to the pace of the cattle that are before me and according to the pace of the children, until I come unto my lord, unto Seir" (Gen. 33:12-14).

Noah was called a *tzadik* (righteous person) because of his extraordinary care of the animals on the ark.[45] He was careful to feed each species its appropriate food at the proper time. He is pictured as being unable to sleep due to his continuous concern for the welfare of the animals.[46] Only one other Torah personality, Joseph, was given the designation *tzadik*. He too provided food for both humans *and animals* in a crisis.

Consistent with the fact that concern for the well-being of animals is the test for a righteous individual, Jacob instructed his son, Joseph, to determine "whether it is well with thy brethren and well with the flock" (Gen. 37:14), and the Israelites in the wilderness besought water for both themselves and their cattle (Num. 20:4).

STORIES FROM THE JEWISH TRADITION RELATED TO COMPASSION TO ANIMALS

> Rabbi Judah, the Prince, was sitting and studying the Torah in front of the Babylonian Synagogue in Sepphoris. A calf being taken to the slaughterhouse came to him as if pleading, "Save me!" Rabbi Judah said to it, "What can I do for you? For this you were created." As a punishment for his heartlessness, he suffered from a toothache for thirteen years.

> One day, a creeping thing (a weasel) ran past Rabbi Judah's daughter who was about to kill it. He said to her, "My daughter, let it be, for it is written, 'and his tender mercies are over all his works' (Ps. 145:9)." Because Rabbi Judah prevented an act of cruelty and unkindness to an animal, his health was restored to him.[47]

Significant in this regard is the response of Ga'on R. Sherira in his *Opinions* to the following inquiry:[48] "If Rabbi Judah was punished because he handed a calf over to the slaughterer, and was once again rewarded because he protected a dumb creature from death, should we learn from this not to slaughter any animal and not to kill harmful animals?" The Ga'on's answer: "Animals that may harm people, such as snakes, lions, wolves, must always be killed; on the other hand, animals that do us no harm and are not needed for food or medicine should not be killed.... To save a calf that we *need* for nourishment is not required of us."[49]

Now that we know that we do *not* need meat for nourishment, and as a matter of fact, the consumption of flesh products harms our health, what a tremendously powerful argument for vegetarianism is in this story and its commentary.

The Maharshah (1555-1631) notes that Rabbi Judah was punished because it was a calf, not a mature animal that had at least tasted life's joys, that was being led to slaughter.[50] This implies that if animals have had a sufficient chance to experience life's pleasures, it would be permissible to slaughter them for food. This again provides a strong argument for vegetarianism for, as discussed in the next section, food animals lack even a moment's happiness as they are raised from birth in closed confined spaces, denied fresh air, sunlight, exercise or emotional attachment.

> Rabbi Israel Salanter, one of the most distinguished Orthodox Rabbis of the nineteenth century, failed to appear one Yom Kippur eve to chant the sacred Kol Nidre Prayer. His congregation became concerned, for it was inconceivable that their saintly rabbi would be late or absent on this very holy day. They sent out a search party to look for him. After much time, their rabbi was found in the barn of a Christian neighbor. On his way to the synagogue, Rabbi Salanter had come upon one of his

neighbor's calves, lost and tangled in the brush. Seeing that the animal was in distress, he freed it and led it home through many fields and over many hills. His act of mercy represented the rabbi's prayers on that Yom Kippur evening.[51]

Rabbi Zusya once was on a journey to collect money to ransom prisoners. He came to an inn and in one room found a large cage with many types of birds. He saw that the birds wanted to fly out of the cage and be free again. He burned with pity for them and said to himself, "Here you are, Zusya, walking your feet off to ransom prisoners. But what greater ransoming of prisoners can there be than to free these birds from their prison?" He then opened the cage, and the birds flew out into freedom.

When the innkeeper saw the empty cage, he was very angry and asked the people in the house who had released the birds. They answered that there was a man loitering around who appeared to be a fool and that he must have done it. The innkeeper shouted at Zusya: "You fool! How could you rob me of my birds and make worthless the good money I paid for them?" Zusya replied: "You have often read these words in the Psalms: 'His tender mercies are over all His work'?" Then the innkeeper beat Zusya until he became tired and then he threw him out of the house. And Zusya went his way serenely.[52]

Rabbi Abramtzi was a man full of compassion—his compassion was for all living things—He would not walk on the grass of the field lest he trample it down. He was very careful not to tread on grasshoppers or crawling insects. If a dog came to the door of his house, he would instruct the members of his household to feed the animal. In winter he would scatter crumbs of bread and seed on the window sills. When sparrows and other birds arrived and began to pick at the food, he could not remove his gaze from them and his face would light up with joy like that of a little child. He looked after his horses far better than his coachmen did. When travelling and the coach had to ascend an incline, he would climb down in order to lighten the load and more often than not he would push the cart from behind.

On summer days he would compel his coachman to stop on the way and turn aside to a field in order that the horses should rest and partake of the grass. The rabbi loved these rest periods in the forest. While the horses were grazing, he would sit under a tree and interest himself in a book. At times he would pray in the field or the forest. This gave him great pleasure, for he used to say, "The field and the forest are the most beautiful and finest of the Houses of the Lord."

It happened once that the rabbi was on the road on a Friday. It would take another three hours to reach home.

Due to the rain the road was very muddy. The wagon could only proceed with difficulty. The mud gripped the wheels and slowed down its progress. It was mid-day and they had not even completed half the journey. The horses were tired and worn out. They had no energy to proceed further.

The rabbi told the driver to stop and give fodder to the horses, so that they could regain their strength. This was done. Afterwards the journey was continued, but the going was heavy and the wagon sunk up to the hubs of the wheels in the mud. In fact it was with the greatest difficulty that the horses maintained their balance in the swampy ground. The vapour of sweat enveloped their skin. Their knees trembled and at any moment they would have to rest. The coachman scolded and urged them on. He then raised his whip on the unfortunate creatures. The rabbi grabbed him by the elbow and cried out: "This is cruelty to animals, cruelty to animals." The coachman answered in fury: "What do you want me to do? Do you want us to celebrate the Sabbath here?"

"What of it?" replied the rabbi quietly. "It is better that we celebrate the Sabbath here than cause the death of these animals by suffering. Are they not the creatures of the Lord? See how exhausted they are. They have not the energy to take one more step forward."

"But what of the Sabbath? How can Jews observe the Sabbath in the forest?" asked the coachman.

"My friend, it does not matter. The Sabbath Queen will come to us also here, for her glory fills the whole world, and particularly in those places where Jews yearn for her. The Lord shall do what is good in His eyes. He will look after us, supply us with our wants and guard us against all evil."[53]

The African King, Kazia was astounded when he observed the cruel and unjust way in which Alexander of Macedonia judged disputes:
King: Does the sun shine in your country?
Alexander: Yes.
King: Perhaps there are small cattle in your country?
Alexander: Yes.
King: It is because of the merit of the small cattle that the sun shines upon you and the rain falls upon you. For the sake of the small cattle you are saved!
The Rabbis commented: Hence it is written, "Man and beast Thou preserved O Lord" (Psalm 36:7), as much to say, "Thou preservest man, O Lord, because of the merit of the beast."[54]

TREATMENT OF ANIMALS TODAY

As we have seen, the Jewish tradition stresses compassion for animals and commands that we strive to avoid causing them pain *(tsa'ar ba'alei chayim)*. Unfortunately, the conditions under which animals are raised for food today are quite different from any the Torah would endorse.

Chickens are raised for slaughter in long, windowless, crowded sheds, where they never see sunlight, breathe fresh air, or get any exercise.[55] From hoppers suspended from the roof, they obtain food and water, along with many chemical additives according to a programmed schedule. Crowding is so bad that chickens cannot even stretch their wings. The results of these very unnatural conditions are potential feather-pecking and cannibalism. To avoid this, the lighting is kept very dim, the chickens are given special contact lenses, and more drastically, they are "de-beaked." De-beaking involves cutting off part of the chicken's beak with a hot knife while its head is held in a guillotine-like device, a very painful process.

Ruth Harrison describes the results of her observations of current methods of raising chickens in her excellent book, *Animal Machines*. She found that the chickens seemed to have lost their minds; their eyes gleamed through the bars, they viciously pecked at any hand within reach, and they pulled feathers out of other chickens' backs looking for flesh and blood to eat.[56]

Because so many birds are killed daily in continuous operations by the vast breeding companies, a prayer which should be recited upon the ritual slaughter of every bird has become a prayer for every thousand birds.

There is tremendous cruelty in the forced feeding of ducks and geese to produce *pate de foie gras*.[57] Foie gras literally means fat liver. The liver of a goose or duck is fattened by having 60 to 80 pounds of corn inserted by force down its gullet. The farmer generally holds the neck of the goose between his legs, pouring the corn with one hand and massaging it down the neck with the other. When this process is no longer effective, a wooden plunger is used to compact it still further. The bird suffers unimaginable pain, and as the liver grows to an enormous size, sclerosis of the liver develops. Finally, after 25 days of such agony, when the bird is completely stupefied with pain and unable to move, it is killed and the gigantic liver, considered a delicacy, is removed. Currently machines are used to force-feed birds to make the process more "efficient," with greater resultant agony.

Unfortunately, Israel today is one of the world's major exporters of pate de foie gras.[58]

Although it would seem impossible to surpass the cruelties described in the previous cases, perhaps this occurs in raising veal calves. After being allowed to nurse for only 1 or 2 days, the veal calf is removed from its mother, with no consideration of its need for motherly nourishment, affection, and physical contact. The calf is locked in a small slotted stall without enough space to move around, stretch, or even lie down. To obtain the pale, tender veal desired by consumers, the calf is purposely kept anemic by giving it a special high-calorie, iron- free diet. The calf craves iron so much that it would lick the iron fittings on its stall and its own urine if permitted to do so; it is prevented from turning by having its head tethered to the stall. The stall is kept very warm and the calf is not given any water, so that it will drink more of its high-calorie liquid diet. The very unnatural conditions of the veal calf - its lack of exercise, sunlight, fresh air, proper food and water and any emotional stimulation make for a very sick, anemic animal. Antibiotics and drugs are used to keep the calf from becoming ill. The calf leaves its pen only when taken for slaughter; sometimes it drops dead from the exertion of going to slaughter.

In a two-part article in the *Jewish Press*,[59] Rabbi A. Spero discusses *halachic* (Jewish law) problems related to current methods of raising veal calves. He points out that animals that are too weak or sick to walk by their own strength are not even suitable for ritual slaughter. He indicates that the horrible conditions under which calves are raised should result in only 30 percent of calves meeting kosher requirements, and that there should be concern with any packing-house yielding consistently higher percentages.

The transportation of animals by rail or truck involves additional cruelties.[60] They are jammed into a confined area for many hours, sometimes days, where they suffer from lack of food, water, exercise, and ventilation. They are often exposed to extreme heat, cold, and humidity. They are generally not fed for the last 24 to 48 hours prior to slaughter.

The inhumane treatment of animals raised for food is summarized in the following two selections:

> How far have we the right to take our domination of the animal world? Have we the right to rob them of all pleasures in life simply to make more money more quickly out of their carcasses? Have we the right to treat living creatures solely as food-converting machines? At what point do we acknowledge cruelty?[61]

> Every year millions of animals are born and bred for the sole purpose of satisfying those who like the taste of meat. Their lives vary in length from a few weeks to a few years; most live a fraction of the time they would in more natural conditions. They die in slaughter-houses where, if the tranquilizers have their effect, they know only a few moments of the awful fear of death before they are stunned, and their throats cut. This is what all meat-eaters actively support, for there would be no batteries, no sweat-boxes, no need to castrate male animals or artificially inseminate females, no cattle markets and no slaughter- houses if there was no one insensitive enough to buy their products. It is simply impossible to farm animals for food without imprisoning, mutilating and eventually slaughtering them, and no one can ignore this price that has to be paid for the pleasure of eating meat.[62]

Ruth Harrison eloquently summarizes how animals are raised today:

> To some extent...farm animals have always been exploited by man in that he rears them specifically for food. But until recently they were individuals, allowed their birthright of green fields, sunlight, and fresh air; they were allowed to forage, to exercise, to watch the world go by, in fact to live. Even at its worst,...the animal had some enjoyment in life before it died. Today the exploitation has been taken to a degree which involves not only the elimination of all enjoyment, the frustration of all natural instincts, but its replacement with acute discomfort, boredom, and the actual denial of health. It has been taken to a degree where the animal is not allowed to live before it dies.[63]

As the previous examples indicate, the conditions under which animals are raised today are completely contrary to the Jewish ideals of compassion and avoiding *tsa'ar ba'alei chayim.* Instead of animals being free to graze on the Sabbath day to enjoy the beauties of creation, they are confined for all of their lives to darkened, crowded cells without air, natural light, or the ability to exercise. Whereas the Torah mandates that animals should be able to eat the products of the harvest as they thresh in the fields, today animals are given chemical fatteners and other additives in their food, based on computer programs. Where Judaism indicates consideration for animals by mandating that a strong and weak animal not be yoked together, veal calves spend their entire lives standing on slats, their necks chained to the sides, without sunlight, fresh air, or exercise.

The pre-eminent 18th-century rabbinic authority, R. Ezekiel Landau asserted that the mere killing of an animal for food does not violate the prohibition against *tsa'ar ba'alei chayim*; this prohibition is only applicable "if he causes (the animal) pain while alive."[64] In view of the horrible conditions under which animals are raised today, it would be difficult to argue that this biblical prohibition is not being severely violated.

Jews who continue to eat meat raised under such conditions would seem to be helping to support a system which is contrary to basic Jewish principles and obligations.

3

Preserving Health and Life

> You may not in any way weaken your health or shorten your life. Only if the body is healthy is it an efficient instrument for the spirit's activity....Therefore you should avoid everything which might possibly injure your health.... And the law asks you to be even more circumspect in avoiding danger to life and limb than in the avoidance of other transgressions. (Rabbi Samson Raphael Hirsch, Horeb[1])

Judaism regards the preservation of physical well-being as a religious command of great importance. Jews are to take care of their health and do nothing that might unnecessarily endanger themselves. Life is regarded as the highest good, and we are obligated to protect it.

An important Jewish principle is pikuach nefesh, the duty to preserve a human life. The talmudic sages applied the principle "Ye shall therefore keep my statutes and ordinances, which if a man do he shall live by them" (Lev. 18:5) to all the laws of the Torah. Hence Jews are to be more particular about matters concerning danger to health and life than about ritual matters.[2] If it could help save a life, one must (not may) violate the Sabbath, eat forbidden foods, and even eat on Yom Kippur.[3] The only laws that cannot be violated to preserve a life are those prohibiting murder, idolatry, and sexual immorality.[4]

According to the Torah, we are not allowed to place ourselves intentionally in danger; it states "take heed to thyself and take care of your lives" (Deut. 4:9) and, again, "take good care of your lives (Deut. 4:15).

The Torah, Talmud, and *Codes of Jewish Law* stress the avoidance of danger through the positive commandment of making a parapet (wall) for one's roof so that no one will fall from the roof (Deut. 22:8). Rabbi Hertz, in his commentary on this commandment, stated that failure to protect human life exposes one to guilt for the spilling of blood, in God's eyes.[5] The talmudic sages extended this prohibition to cover all cases where negligence endangers life, such as placing a broken ladder against a wall or keeping a dangerous dog.[6]

In his classic Mishneh Torah, Maimonides indicates a variety of prohibitions, all based on the necessity to do everything possible to preserve life:

> It makes no difference whether it be one's roof or anything else that is dangerous and might possibly be a stumbling block to someone and cause his death—for example, if one has a well or a pit, with or without water, in his yard—the owner is obliged to build an enclosing wall ten handbreadths high, or else to put a cover over it lest someone fall into it and be killed. Similarly, regarding any obstacle which is dangerous to life, there is a positive commandment to remove it and to beware of it, and to be particularly careful in this matter, for Scripture says, "Take heed unto thyself and take care of thy life" (Deut. 4:9). If one does not remove dangerous obstacles and allows them to remain, he disregards a positive commandment and transgresses the prohibition: *Thou bring not blood* (Deut. 22:8).
>
> Many things are forbidden by the Sages because they are dangerous to life. If one disregards any of these and says, "If I want to put myself in danger, what concern is it to others?" or "I am not particular about such things," he must be disciplined.
>
> The following are prohibited acts: One may not put his mouth to a flowing pipe of water and drink from it, or drink at night from rivers or ponds, lest he swallow a leech while unable to see. Nor may one drink water that has been left uncovered, lest he drink from it after a snake or other poisonous reptile has drunk from it, and die.[7]

Maimonides' statements clearly indicate that Judaism absolutely prohibits the placing of one's health or life into possible danger. He disallows the popular rationalization, "What concern is it to others if I endanger myself?"

There are similar prohibitions against endangering one's life in the *Shulchan Aruch* of Rabbi Joseph Caro (1488-1575) and other Codes of Jewish Law.[8] In Choshen Mishpat 427, Caro devotes an entire chapter to "the positive commandment of removing any object or obstacle which constitutes a danger to life." In his glossary on Caro's *Shulchan Aruch*, Rabbi Moses Isserles (the Rema) concludes:

> One should avoid all things that might lead to danger because a danger to life is stricter than a prohibition. One should be more concerned about a possible danger to life than a possible prohibition. Therefore, the Sages prohibited one to walk in a place of danger such as near a leaning wall (for fear of collapse), or alone at night (for fear of robbers). They also prohibited drinking water from rivers at night ... because these things may lead to danger ... and he who is concerned with his health [lit.: watches his soul] avoids them. And it is prohibited to rely on a miracle or to put one's life in danger by any of the aforementioned or the like.[9]

The Talmud tells that Rabbi Huna, a great Torah authority, would personally inspect all the walls of his town of Sura before the onset of the winter storms. Any walls that he found unsafe, he would order torn down. If the owner could not afford to rebuild the wall, Rabbi Huna would pay for it from his own funds.[10]

Life is considered so sacred in Judaism that the tradition asserts that "if a person saves one life, it is as if he or she saved an entire world".[11] The preservation of human life is so important that it takes precedence over acts of reverence for a dead person, even if that person is a leader or great hero: "For a one day-old child (that is dangerously ill), the Sabbath may be profaned...; for David, King of Israel, once he is dead the Sabbath must not be profaned".[12] Also, one must sooner rescue from flames any living infant than the dead body of one's own parent.[13]

Rabbinic literature is specific in its stress on proper hygiene to protect health. The human body is considered as a sanctuary.[14] The importance of good and regular meals is stressed[15], and the rabbis give much advice on foods conducive to health[16]. They stress the importance of personal cleanliness and washing daily in honor of God.[17] The talmudic sage Hillel considered it a religious commandment to bathe in order to protect his health.[18]

As will be discussed in detail in chapter 5, the Jewish sages prohibit the unnecessary destruction of anything of value. The extension of this prohibition to include the willful destruction of one's own body is made by Rabbi Israel Lipshuetz, (died 1782), known as *Tifereth Yisroel*.[19]

Rabbi Samson Raphael Hirsch, in *Horeb*, in his analysis of the commandments, writes very powerfully of the mandate to preserve health and life:

> Limiting our presumption against our own body, God's word calls to us: "Do not commit suicide!" "Do not injure yourself!" "Do not ruin yourself!" "Do not weaken yourself!" "Preserve yourself!"[20]

Suicide, whether rapid or slow, is prohibited in Jewish law. This is, as indicated earlier, based on the Torah phrase, "and surely your blood, the blood of your lives, will I require" (Gen. 9:5). As will be discussed later in this section, there is evidence showing that eating meat constitutes a form of slow suicide.

People use a number of arguments to justify the continuance of a dangerous habit, such as smoking, or to mitigate against the imposition of a rabbinic ban on such habits, based on Jewish law. But in every case, these arguments can be rejected in the face of *pikuach nefesh*, the requirement to preserve human life.[21]

The preceding discussions indicate that if it can be clearly and convincingly shown that the consumption of meat is dangerous to people's health, it should be prohibited by Jewish law.

RESULTS WHEN PEOPLE HAVE LIVED UNDER VEGETARIAN DIETS

During World War I, Denmark was cut off from its meat supply because of a blockade by the Allied forces. To avoid acute food shortages, the government sought the aid of Denmark's vegetarian society. Dr. Mikkel Hindhede wrote about the results in the *Journal of the American Medical Association*. He pointed out that only the wealthy could afford to buy meat, and most of the population ate bran, bread, barley, porridge, potatoes, greens, milk, and some butter.[22] This nearly vegetarian diet led to better health and reduced mortality rates (17%) for the Danish people during the first year of the new diet.[23]

A similar occurrence happened in Norway when food rationing was instituted during World War II and the consumption of meat was sharply cut. Because of the reduction in animal fats consumed, the Norwegian death rate dropped from 31 per 10,000 people in 1938 to about 20 per 10,000 people in 1944.[24] After the war, when the prewar diets resumed, the mortality rate rose sharply, reaching 26 per 10,000 people in 1946.[25]

Unlike the short wartime experiences of the Danes and Norwegians, many Seventh-Day Adventists have followed a vegetarian diet for over 100 years. They also abstain from smoking, alcohol, coffee, tea, spices, hot condiments, and highly refined foods. A recent study of their health shows that colonic, rectal, and intestinal cancer are 50-70% lower than in the general population.[26]

In another study of Seventh-Day Adventist women, about half of whom were vegetarian, lower blood pressure and a rate of endometrial cancer 40% lower than women in the general population were found.[27]

An Australian study found the blood pressures of Seventh-Day Adventist vegetarians between 30-79 years of age, to be "significantly less" that the levels found in nonvegetarian controls.[28] The study concludes that dietary factors, probably intake of animal protein, animal fat, or another dietary component associated with them, are likely to be responsible for the differences in blood-pressure readings.[29]

After studying the mainly vegetarian diet of the Hunzas of Kashmir, noted for their longevity, Major-General Sir Robert McCarrison, once physician to the king of England, stated: "I never saw a case of asthenic dyspepsia, of gastric or duodenal ulcer, of appendicitis, or mucus colitis or cancer."[30]

Dr. Paul Dudley White, the famous heart specialist, visited the Hunzas in 1964. His studies show that the 90- and 110-year- old men tested showed no evidence of heart disease. He stated that there is a correlation between their diet and lifestyles and the low incidence of heart disease.[31]

The Bible contains an interesting case of people eating only vegetarian foods. The Book of Daniel tells how Daniel and his three companions were captives in the court of Nebuchadnezzar, king of Babylon. They refused to defile themselves with the king's meat and wine, which were not kosher. The king's servant was fearful that their health would suffer and the king would blame him. But Daniel said: "For ten days, give us pulse (peas, beans, and lentils) to eat and water to drink. Then let our countenances be looked upon before thee, and the countenance of those children that eat of the portion of the king's meat; and as thou seeth, deal with thy servants." The king's servant consented to wait the period and "at the end of the ten days their countenances appeared fairer and fatter in flesh than all the children who did eat the portion of the king's meat." The king's servant then took away from the others their meat and wine and fed them also pulse and water (Dan. 1:8-16).

ILLNESSES RELATED TO MEAT CONSUMPTION

(a) HEART DISEASE

Medical authorities are finding increasing evidence linking arteriosclerosis, a thickening of the walls of arteries associated with heart attacks and strokes, to meat-centered diets, which are high in saturated fats and cholesterol. The American Heart Association has stated:

> Studies have indicated that many people who show no evidence of heart disease are increasing their risk of heart attack by following a diet that is high in saturated fat and cholesterol. The typical American diet ... tends to raise the level of cholesterol in the blood, and a high blood cholesterol contributes to the development of arteriosclerosis.[32]

A recent cover story in *Time* magazine[33] indicated the negative effects of the American diet on heart problems. The following are just a few of their many significant statements:

1) The U.S. continues to have one of the highest rates of heart disease in the world. According to the National Heart, Lung, and Blood Institute, heart attacks in 1983 cost the nation about $60 billion in medical bills, lost wages, and productivity, or more than the total Medicare budget for that year.

2) Dr. Charles Glueck, director of the University of Cincinnati Lipid Research Center, one of twelve centers that participated in a study

relating cholesterol levels to heart attacks, concludes, "For every 1% reduction in total cholesterol level, there is a 2% reduction of heart disease risk."

3) Columbia University Cardiologist, Robert Levy, a director of a similar study, says, "If we can get everyone to lower his cholesterol level 10% to 15% by cutting down on fat and cholesterol in the diet, heart attack deaths in this country will decrease by 20% to 30%.

Statistics indicate that populations of countries where meat consumption is high (such as the United States, Canada, and Australia) have high mortality rates from heart disease. Populations of developed countries with the lowest meat consumption (Italy and Japan) have considerably lower mortality rates from heart disease.[34]

The negative effects of meat consumption start early. A study of American men, ages 19-22, killed in the Korean War showed a high degree of arteriosclerosis, compared with similar-aged Koreans, who were relatively free of this disease.[35] Although the Koreans were then basically vegetarians, the American diet consisted largely of milk, butter, eggs, and meat.

In 1970, an Inter-Society Commission for Heart Disease Resources, composed of 29 voluntary health agencies including the American Medical Association, investigated what the American public should do to stem the "epidemic" of arteriosclerosis and heart attacks. A key recommendation was that there should be less meat in the diet so that there would be reductions of dietary cholesterol, dietary saturated fat, and total fat. They also recommended that the diet contain more fruits, vegetables, grains, and legumes.[36]

In 1977, an important document, *Dietary Goals for the United States*, was adopted and published by a Senate Select Committee on Nutrition and Human Needs. They also recommended that the American diet have less cholesterol, saturated fat, and total fat, that the consumption of red meat be reduced, and that there be added consumption of whole grains, fruits, and vegetables.[37]

The last two studies cited indicate that top scientific and political groups are stressing the need for improved diets, with less red meat and increased consumption of vegetarian foods.

Based on a variety of scientific studies, Dr. John A. Scharffenberg, an associate professor of applied nutrition and a director of a community health education program concludes that proper diets can reduce serum cholesterol and thus arteriosclerosis, which would decrease mortality rates from coronary heart disease.[38] He suggests, consistent with the previously discussed studies, that people adopt a "prudent diet," one low in fat, meat, and cholesterol and high in fruits, whole grains, vegetables, and legumes.

Nutritionist Nathan Pritikin, founder of the Longevity Centre and Longevity Research Institute in California, felt that Jews can reduce heart disease, hypertension, and other diseases by switching to a low-fat, low-protein, high-carbohydrate diet. He claimed that "the average Jewish diet must have been designed by the enemies of the Jewish people."[39]

(b) CANCER

Cancer is America's second leading cause of death, right behind diseases of the heart and blood vessels. One out of every 3 Americans will get cancer during their lifetimes, and over 60 percent who do will die from the disease within 5 years.[40]

There have been several recent studies in the United States and other countries aimed at investigating whether there is a connection between meat eating and various forms of cancer. In 1975, at the Symposia on Nutrition in the Causation of Cancer, Dr. Ernest L. Wydner stated that dietary factors could be related to as much as 50% of all cancers found in women and a third of all cancers found in men.[41]

Breast Cancer . There is evidence that shows a positive correlation between a diet heavy in animal fats and the incidence of breast cancer.[42] Most breast cancers are found in the populations of countries where people eat large amounts of animal fat, such as the United States, Great Britain, Australia, Argentina, and Canada. In countries where little animal fat, particularly beef, is consumed, breast cancer rates are extremely low. European Jewish women living in Israel are three times more likely to get breast cancer than Asian or Oriental Jews. Japanese women in the United States are four times more likely to develop breast cancer than their counterparts in Japan.[43]

Cancer of the Colon.. It took President Reagan's problems with colon cancer to put a spotlight on the link between diet and colon cancer.

Recently the National Cancer Institute and the American Cancer Society have pointed out this connection and have advised dietary changes to prevent this disease.

Several studies have shown that diets highest in animal fats and cholesterol coincide with the highest rate of colon cancer[44], while other studies conclude that a low-fat, high fiber diet prevents it.[45]

Dr. Frey Ellis, a consultant hematologist at Kingston Hospital, Surrngland, states "Cancer of the colon is 20 times more common in meat eaters than in people who eat a lot of vegetables."[46] He suggests that the difference is due to transit time through the bowel: 3 or 4 days for meat compared to 24 hours for vegetable foods, which are high in fiber content.[47]

(c) KIDNEY DISEASE

The consumption of meat creates more waste products, hence more strain on the kidneys. Dr. John H. Kellogg did a comparative analysis of the issue of low protein feeders and those who had an ordinary diet in the 1920's. He found that "even moderate meat eaters require of their kidneys three times the amount of work in elimination of nitrogenous wastes that is demanded of flesh abstainers".[48] He concluded that when kidneys are relatively young they are usually able to handle the extra burden without injury, but as they become older, "they become unable to do their work efficiently."[49] A recent study at Brigham and Williams Hospital in Boston indicated that low-protein, largely vegetarian diets could stop relatively advanced kidney disease in some patients.[50]

Kidney disease is one of the nation's biggest killers. People who suffer from chronic kidney disorders are often treated with a dialysis machine, which aids the kidneys in removing waste products from the blood. Such people can significantly increase the time between treatments through a flesh-free diet.[51]

(d) FOOD POISONING

Over one million cases of food poisoning are reported every year in the United States. Salmonella organisms are responsible in most instances. Meat and poultry products are the usual vehicles of contamination. Vegetarians are rarely bothered by these seldom fatal, but often incapacitating, illnesses.[52] A CBS "60 Minutes" program (Sept. 6, 1987) revealed that 35% of commercial chickens have been found to be carriers of salmonella bacteria.

(e) OTHER DISEASES

In addition to the diseases already discussed, a whole family of other diseases have been linked to the excessive protein, fat, and cholesterol, and the lack of fiber associated with meat-centered diets. Several books, such as *A Vegetarian Sourcebook* and *Living Health* (see the bibliography) cite a wide variety of medical studies relating this diet to diseases such as osteoporosis, gallstones, kidney stones, gout, rheumatoid arthritis, and constipation.

REASONS WHY EATING MEAT IS HARMFUL

(a) WHAT IS OUR "NATURAL" DIET?

There has been much controversy recently over the diet most suitable to people. We will first present the arguments of those who feel that human beings are not naturally suited for a diet that includes flesh.

The French naturalist Baron Cuvier stated: "Fruits, roots, and the succulent parts of vegetables appear to be the natural food of man."[53] Geoffrey Hodson quoted the great Swedish naturalist Linnaeus as follows: "Man's structure, external and internal, compared with the of other animals, shows that fruit and succulent vegetables constitute his natural food."[54] The following comparisons support these statements:[55]

(1) Our small and large intestines, like those of other primates, are four times longer than those of carnivores. Because of the long intestines, meat passes very slowly through the human digestive system; it takes about 4 days during which the disease-causing products of decaying meat are in constant contact with the digestive organs (vegetarian food takes only about 1 1/2 days).[56]

(2) Our hands are similar to those of apes; they are meant for picking food such as vegetables, fruits, leaves, flowers, seeds, etc., and not for tearing flesh.

(3) Our lower jaw, or mandible, can move both up and down and side

to side, like the primates'; carnivores' jaws move only up and down.

(4) Our saliva is alkaline like that of the higher species of apes; it contains ptyalin to digest carbohydrates. Carnivores' saliva is acidic.

(5) Unlike carnivores, we do not have fangs for biting into flesh. Our so-called canine teeth are not truly canine like the dog's. We are not constituted to prey upon animals, rip apart their bodies, or bite into their flesh.

(6) Although our gastric secretions are acidic like that of carnivores, their stomachs have four times as much acid; this strong acidic region is necessary to digest their high-protein flesh diet.

(7) Carnivores have proportionally larger kidneys and livers than we have; they need these larger organs in order to handle the excessive nitrogenous waste of a flesh diet.

(8) The carnivores' livers secrete a far greater amount of bile into the gut to deal with their high-fat meat diet.

Table I indicates that people are closest in structure to animals that primarily eat fruits.

That our natural instinct is not toward flesh food is stated by R. H. Wheldon:

> The gorge of a cat, for instance, will rise at the smell of a mouse or a piece of raw flesh, but not at the aroma of fruit. If a man can take delight in pouncing upon a bird, tear its still living body apart with his teeth, sucking the warm blood, one might infer that Nature had provided him with carnivorous instinct, but the very thought of doing such a thing makes him shudder. On the other hand, a bunch of luscious grapes makes his mouth water, and even in the absence of hunger, he will eat fruit to gratify taste.[57]

Some scientists disagree with the above analysis. They assert that people's natural diet is omnivorous, based on both flesh and vegetarian foods. They point to the many years that our ancestors have eaten meat and the fact that primates, the animals whose systems are closest to ours, have been observed to eat meat.

TABLE I

Structural Comparison of Humans to Animals

Meat eater	*Leaf-grass eater*	*Fruit eater*	*Human beings*
Has claws	No claws	No claws	No claws
No pores on skin; perspires through tongue to cool body	Perspires through millions of pores on skin	Perspires through millions of pores on skin	Perspires through millions of pores on skin
Sharp, pointed front teeth to tear flesh	No sharp, pointed front teeth	No sharp, pointed front teeth	No sharp, pointed front teeth
Small salivary glands in the mouth (not needed to predigest grains and fruits)	Well-developed salivary glands, needed to predigest grains and fruits	Well-developed salivary glands, needed to predigest grains and fruits	Well-developed salivary glands, needed to predigest grains and fruits
Acid saliva; no enzyme ptyalin to predigest grains	Alkaline saliva; much ptyalin to predigest grains	Alkaline saliva; much ptyalin to predigest grains	Alkaline saliva; much ptyalin to predigest grains
No flat, back molar teeth to grind food	Flat, back molar teeth to grind food	Flat, back molar teeth to grind food	Flat, back molar teeth to grind food
Much strong hydrochloric acid in stomach to digest tough animal muscle, bone, etc.	Stomach acid 20 times weaker than meat eaters	Stomach acid 20 times weaker than meat eaters	Stomach acid 20 times weaker than meat eaters

Intestinal tract only 3 times body length so rapidly decaying meat can pass out of body quickly	Intestinal tract 10 times body length; leaf and grains do not decay as quickly and can pass more slowly through the body	Intestinal tract 12 times body length; fruits do not decay as rapidly and can pass more slowly through the body	Intestinal tract 12 times body length

SOURCE: Barbara Parham What's Wrong with Eating Meat? Denver Colo., Ananda Marga Publications, 1979, p. 23. Reproduced with permission.
In response:

(1) Certainly people have eaten meat for at least thousands of years. As indicated, according to the Torah, after first giving people a vegetarian diet (Genesis 1:29), as a concession to human weakness, God gave people permission to eat meat in the time of Noah (Genesis 9:3). Just as an automobile will travel on a fuel which is not most suitable to it, people can live on a diet that is not ideal. The issue is not what people eat now and have eaten in the past, but the diet that is healthiest for people and is most consistent with our anatomy, physiology, and instincts. It should also be noted that a significant portion of people throughout history either ate no meat at all or ate it only on rare occasions. In addition, meat contains no essential nutrients that cannot be obtained from plant sources.

(2) With regard to primates eating meat, this issue has been hotly debated. Some species have never been observed to do so. Jane Goodall's studies of apes showed that meat eating incidents were extremely rare, and they were unusual and atypical of the species in general, occurring in un-chimplike surroundings. The staple diet of primates is vegetarian.

[(A detailed analysis of this entire issue can be found in chapter 3, "The Aberrant Ape", in *Food for a Future* by Jon Wynne-Tyson (Abacus Press, 1976).]

Even if people are naturally omnivorous, this means that we have a choice in our diet in terms of whether or not to eat meat. And it still leaves all the ethical arguments - compassion for animals, helping the hungry, protecting the environment - on the side of vegetarianism. Also, if we define our "natural" diet as that which is best for our health, the abundant evidence in this and many other books point to vegetarianism as our natural diet.

(b) CONDITIONS UNDER WHICH ANIMALS ARE RAISED TODAY

The terrible conditions under which animals are raised today lead to unhealthy animals, which result in poor health for people. In the foreword to Ruth Harrison's book *Animal Machines*, Rachel Carson states:

> As a biologist whose special interest lies in the field of ecology, or the relation between living things and their environment, I find it inconceivable that healthy animals can be produced under the artificial and damaging conditions that prevail in the modern factory- like installations, where animals are grown and turned out like so many inanimate objects. The crowding of broiler chickens, the revolting unsanitary conditions in the piggeries, the lifelong confinement of laying hens in tiny cages... This artificial environment is not a healthy one. Diseases sweep through these establishments, which indeed are kept going only by the continuous administrations of antibiotics. Disease organisms then become resistant to the antibiotics.... The menace to human consumers from the drugs, hormones, and pesticides used to keep this whole fantastic operation somehow going is a matter never fully explored.[58]

Exercise is a must for animals in their natural state. When animals are denied exercise (as generally occurs today with modern factory methods), their complete metabolism is influenced. Their meat becomes infested with waste (metabolism poison), which would have disappeared had the animals been permitted to exercise.[59]

Other factors that negatively affect human health are hormones, tranquilizers, antibiotics, which are administered to animals, radioactive substances, which they ingest with their food, and sodium nitrate, sodium nitrite, and sodium sulfite, which are used as antispoilage agents in many prepared meats. These agents have all been shown to have negative health effects.[60]

Just before and during slaughter, the terrified animal's biochemistry changes profoundly. The entire carcass is pain- poisoned by toxic by-products that are forced throughout the body. Large amounts of hormones, especially adrenalin, remain in the meat and later enter and poison human tissue. The Nutrition Institute of America has stated, "The flesh of an animal carcass is loaded with toxic blood and other waste by-products."[61]

(c) NEGATIVE EFFECTS OF PESTICIDES

Pesticides and other pollutants increase to serious proportions as we move up the food chain. The following is the potential build-up of a pollutant in a food chain, starting with one unit of pollution in water.[62]

1	—water	
10	—phytoplankton	microscopic organisms
100	—zooplankton	
1,000	—shrimps	
10,000	—small fish	
100,000	—medium fish	
1,000,000	—large fish	
10,000,000	—chicken living on fish meal	

At each ascending level of the food chain, the effect of the pollutant is magnified about ten times. One unit of pollution in water can be increased by a factor of millions by the end of a food chain. Hence the concentration of environmental poisons is many times larger in meat and fish than in vegetarian foods.

According to an exhibit at the Ontario Science Museum in Toronto, the build up of DDT is: 0.04 parts per million (ppm) in algae; 0.28 ppm in a fish or eel; and 13.3 ppm is a fish-eating osprey.

This huge magnification of pollutants as one consumes food higher on food chain has led to some concern about dangerous chemicals being transmitted from nursing mothers to their infants. Numerous studies have shown that breast feeding has many positive benefits for both mothers and babies. It is the best food for the baby, since it has all the necessary nutrients, decreases the chances for allergies, and represents the only completely adequate food for the first 6 months.[63]

However, a recent study by the United States Environmental Protection Agency of 1,400 women in 46 states found widespread contamination with such dangerous substances as DDT, dieldrin, and PCB in mothers' milk. The Environmental Defense Fund has published a booklet called "Birthright Denied: The Risks' and Benefits of Breast Feeding,"[64] in which it indicates that in many cases the amount of these chemicals in breast milk is well above levels regarded as safe. The group advises women who are contemplating nursing their babies to have their breast milk tested.

Vegetarian women have been found to have one-third to one-half the levels of pesticides of women having nonvegetarian diets. A young woman considering nursing her child should strongly consider these findings. Because breast feeding has so many benefits, a shift toward a vegetarian diet would be a major step toward healthier babies, as well as healthier mothers.

In an interview, Stephanie Harris of the Environmental Defense Fund states:

> If you're a heavy meat consumer we recommend you nurse once a day and supplement with bottle feeding. But if your diet is—and has been—very low in animal fats, one can assume that the residues in your body will be lower; the benefits of breast feeding will then outweigh the risks....If you're planning on becoming pregnant and especially if you plan on nursing, then become a vegetarian or reduce your consumption of animal fats by other dietary methods.[65]

For more information on breast feeding, you may write to La Leche League, 9619 Minneapolis Avenue, Franklin Park, Illinois 60131, or to the Environmental Defense Fund, 1616 P Street, N.W., Washington, D. C. 20077.

(d) NEGATIVE EFFECTS OF ANTIBIOTICS

Nearly half of the 25 million pounds of antibiotics produced in the U. S. are fed to livestock.[66] These drugs are used because they reduce disease and increase the weight gain of animals. Use of the antibiotics has increased 400 percent in the last 20 years.[67] Since the 1970's, several European countries have banned the use of certain antibiotics in livestock feeds, but no restrictions exist in the U.S., although the Food and Drug Administration has agreed to hold hearings on the issue.

The U. S. Office of Technology Assessment, an arm of Congress, recently concluded[68] that the massive use of antibiotics such as tetracycline and penicillin in animal feeds is making bacteria more resistant, with increasing danger to human health. The health risk results when the drugs prove ineffective when used in patients. The problem occurs because, as antibiotics are ingested when consuming flesh, the predominant susceptible strains of bacteria are overcome. Then the more resistant, formerly uncommon strains of bacteria become dominant and once-effective drugs no longer work. In a letter to the New York Times (Jan. 3, 1978), Werner K. Maas, Professor of Microbiology at the New York University Medical Center, indicated that his studies verified the above conclusions.

(e) INADEQUACY OF INSPECTION

Inspectors must inspect 20,000 or more chickens a day at a rate of up to 70 birds a minute, under conditions involving a 90-decibel roar and a drizzle of blood and flying entrails. Some inspectors complain of an assembly line affliction called "line hypnosis." They lose concentration and awareness; the birds become a blurred yellow vision, and some bad ones inevitably slip through.[69]

Extended discussion of the inadequacies of meat inspection can be found in *Animal Factories* by Jim Mason and *Modern Meat* by Orville Schell. They clearly indicate the failures of government inspection.

CONCLUSION

Medical and statistical evidence demonstrates that the eating of flesh is hazardous to health and can lead to fatal diseases. In this regard it is significant that Rabbi Alfred Cohen concludes his comprehensive article, "Vegetarianism From a Jewish Perspective", with this statement:

> Following the many precedents prescribed in the *Code of Jewish Law*, we would have little difficulty in arriving at the conclusion that, if indeed eating meat is injurious to one's health, it is not only permissible, but possibly even mandatory that we reduce our ingestion of an unhealthful product to the minimal level.[70]

In view of the recent high number of degenerative diseases among the Jewish people, the numerous halachic rules prohibiting dangerous activities should be extended to include the eating of flesh. Such an extension by leading rabbinic authorities of our time, preferably acting jointly and with proper publicity, would save many lives and improve the health and life expectancy of the Jewish people.

4

Feeding the Hungry

> If one takes seriously the moral, spiritual, and humanitarian values of biblical, prophetic, and rabbinic Judaism, the inescapable issue of conscience that must be faced is: How can anyone justify not becoming involved in trying to help save the lives of starving millions of human beings throughout the world—whose plight constitutes the most agonizing moral and humanitarian problem in the latter half of the 20th century.
>
> Rabbi Marc H. Tannenbaum National Interreligious Affairs Director of the American Jewish Committee[1]

JUDAISM ON HUNGER

On Yom Kippur, the holiest day of the Jewish year, while fasting and praying for a good year, Jews are told through the words of the Prophet Isaiah that fasting and prayers are not sufficient; they must work to end oppression and provide food for needy people:

> Is not this the fast that I have chosen? To loose the chains of wickedness, to undo the bonds of oppression, and to let the oppressed go free.... Is it not to share thy bread with the hungry? (Isa. 58:6-7)

Helping the hungry is fundamental in Judaism. The Talmud states, "Providing charity for poor and hungry people weighs as heavily as all the other commandments of the Torah combined."[2] The *Midrash* teaches:

> God says to Israel, "My children, whenever you give sustenance to the poor, I impute it to you as though you gave sustenance to Me...." Does then God eat and drink? No, but whenever you give food to the poor, God accounts it to you as if you gave food to Him.[3]

On Passover we are reminded not to forget the poor. Besides providing *ma'ot chittim* (charity for purchasing matzah) for the needy before Passover, at the seders, we reach out to them:

> This is the bread of affliction which our
> ancestors ate in the land of Egypt.
> Let all who are hungry come and eat. Let all who are in need come and celebrate the Passover.[4]

We are even admonished to feed our enemies, if they are in need:

> If your enemy is hungry, give him bread to eat. If your enemy is thirsty, give him water to drink. (Prov. 25:21)

This is consistent with the Jewish teaching that the greatest hero is a person who converts an enemy into a friend (Avot de Rabbi Nathan, chapter 23).

It is a basic Jewish belief that God provides enough for all. In our daily prayers, it is said, "He openeth up his hand and provideth sustenance to all living things" (Ps. 145:16). Jews are obligated to give thanks to God for providing enough food for us and for all of humanity. In the *bircat hamazon* (grace after meals), we thank God "who feeds the whole world with goodness, grace, loving kindness, and tender mercy."

The blessing is correct. God *has* provided enough for all. The bounties of nature, if properly distributed and properly consumed, would sustain all people. Millions of people are hungry today, not because of insufficient agricultural capacity, but because of unjust social systems and wasteful methods of food production, including the feeding of tremendous amounts of grains to animals to fatten them for slaughter.

WORLD HUNGER TODAY

World hunger statistics are staggering: Over 1 billion people, nearly a quarter of the world's population, are chronically undernourished.[5] Between 700 and 800 million people lack sufficient income to obtain the basic necessities of life.[6] Fifteen to twenty million people die annually due to hunger and its effects, including diseases brought on by lowered resistance due to malnutrition.[7]

Children are particularly victimized by malnutrition. Three out of four who die due to hunger are children. In poor countries, over 40 percent of all deaths occur among children under five years old.[8] Over 8 percent of the world's children die before their first birthday.[9] At least 100,000 children annually go blind due to vitamin A deficiency in their diet. Malnourishment also brings listlessness and reduced capacity for learning and activities, which perpetuates the legacy of poverty.

These startling statistics may make us forget the effects of hunger on one individual:

> Hunger feels like pincers, like the bite of crabs,
> it burns, burns, and has no fire. Hunger is a cold fire....
> For now I ask no more than the justice of eating.[10]

The extensive hunger and malnutrition in so many parts of the world make rebellion and violence more likely. Professor Georg Borgstrom, internationally known expert on food science, fears that "the rich world is on a direct collision course with the poor of the world.... We cannot survive behind our Maginot line of missiles and bombs."[11] Hence the outlook for global stability is very poor, unless the problem of global hunger is soon solved. Professor Robert Heilbroner, the noted economist, predicted that, in times of severe famine, countries like India will be sorely tempted to try nuclear blackmail.[12]

One important reason why many are starving today is that tremendous amount of grains are used to fatten animals for slaughter. Meat-centered diets are very wasteful of grain, land, water, fuel, and fertilizer.

It takes about 16 pounds of grain to produce one pound of edible beef in a feedlot. Half of U.S. farm acreage is used to produce feed crops for livestock. A meat-centered diet requires about seventeen times the land area per person than would be required for a purely vegetarian diet. Animal agriculture also requires tremendous inputs of chemical fertilizer and pesticides, irrigation water, and fuel - commodities which are becoming very scarce worldwide.[13]

Not only is much land and many resources used in the United States to raise beef, but the United States is also the world's largest importer of beef.[14] We import approximately 1 million head of cattle every year from Mexico, half as much beef as all Mexicans have left for themselves.[15] In spite of widespread poverty and malnutrition in Honduras, they export large amounts of beef to the United States. Beef for export in Honduras is grown by a tiny wealthy elite (0.3% of the total population) who own over 25% of all cultivable land.[16]

Research at the Institute for Food and Development in California has shown that the world produces enough grain to provide every person with sufficient protein and about 3,000 calories a day, about the average American's caloric intake.[17] The 3,000-calorie estimate does not include fruits, vegetables, nuts, root crops, and non-grain-fed meat produced by the world's people.

Georg Borgstrom, author of *The Hungry Planet*, points out that protein-starved underdeveloped countries actually export more protein to wealthy nations than they receive. He calls this "the protein swindle." Ninety percent of the world's fish meal catch, for example, is exported to rich countries. Borgstrom states:

> Sometimes one wonders how many Americans and western Europeans have grasped the fact that quite a few of their beef steaks, quarts of milk, dozens of eggs, and hundreds of broilers are the result, not of their agriculture, but of the approximately two million metric tons of protein, mostly of high quality, which astute Western businessmen channel away from the needy and hungry.[18]

Grains are increasingly being fed to livestock in the third world, although the majority of people there can't afford to eat meat.[19] Much of the best land in poorer countries is used to graze livestock, often for export. In Central America, two-thirds of the agriculturally productive land is used for livestock production, for the wealthy or for export.[20]

The wastefulness of flesh-centered diets also affects the Soviet Union. While they produce enough grain to feed their own people plus all of Africa and Europe, a growing demand for meat has led them to feed their own grain and imported soybeans to animals, with the result that they have had to import U.S. wheat to feed the Soviet people.[21]

JEWISH RESPONSES TO HUNGER

1. INVOLVEMENT

Judaism teaches involvement and concern with the plight of fellow human beings. Every life is sacred, and we are obligated to do what we can to help others. The Torah states, "Thou shalt not stand idly by the blood of thy brother" (Lev. 19:16).

We speak out justifiably against the silence of the world when 6 million Jews and 5 million other people were murdered in the Holocaust. Can we be silent when millions die agonizing deaths because of lack of food? Can we acquiesce to the apathy of the world to the fate of starving people?

Elie Wiesel has pointed out that there can be no analogies to the Holocaust, but that it can be used as a reference. In that context, we can consider both the 10 million infants who die each year due to malnutrition and the 6 million Jews who were slaughtered by the Nazis. True, victims of hunger are not being singled out because of their religion, race, or nationality, but, like the Holocaust victims, they die while the world goes about its business, grumbling about "soaring inflation" and personal inconveniences, indifferent to the plight of the starving masses. And yet the Talmud teaches that if one saves a single human life, it is as if one has saved a whole world. What then if one permits a single life to perish? Or 10 million?

The Hebrew prophets berated those who were content and comfortable while others were in great distress:

> *Tremble you women who are at ease,*
> *Shudder you complacent ones;*
> *Strip and make yourselves bare,*
> *Gird sackcloth upon your loins.* (Isa. 32:11)

Woe to those who are at ease in Zion....
Woe to those who lie upon beds of ivory
And stretch themselves upon their couches....
Who drink wine from bowls
And anoint themselves with the finest oils
But are not grieved at the ruin of Joseph.

(Amos 6:1,4,6)

Like other peoples, Jews have frequently experienced hunger. Because of famines, Abraham was forced to go to Egypt (Gen. 12:10), Isaac went to the land of Avimelech, king of the Philistines, in Gerar (Gen. 26:1), the children of Jacob went to Egypt to buy grain (Gen. 42:1-3), and Naomi and her family fled Israel and went to Moab (Ruth 1:1-2). There were also famines in the reigns of King David (2 Sam. 21:1) and King Ahab (1 Kings 18:1-2).

Jews know the sorrow of great hunger. The Prophet Jeremiah states: Happier were the victims of the sword than the victims of hunger, who pined away, stricken by want of the yield of the field (Lam. 4:9).

Based on Jewish values and Jewish history, we must identify with the starving masses of the world. We must be involved by speaking out and acting. Some traditional Jewish ways to help needy people are to pursue justice, practice charity, reduce poverty, show compassion, share resources, and simplify lifestyles.

2. PURSUING JUSTICE

The pursuit of a just society, is one of the most fundamental concepts of Judaism. Note two things about the following important statement in Deuteronomy (16:20): "Justice, justice shalt thou pursue." First, the word "justice" is repeated. This is a very infrequent occurrence in the Torah. When words are repeated, it is generally to add emphasis. Second, we are told to pursue justice. Hence we are not to wait for the right opportunity, the right time and place, but are to *pursue* or run after opportunities to practice justice.

King Solomon asserts:

> *To do righteousness and justice is preferred by*
> *God above sacrifice* (Prov. 21:3)

The psalmist writes: "Give justice to the weak and the fatherless; maintain the right of the afflicted and the destitute" (Ps. 82:3-4).

The prophet Amos cries out that God does not only want sacrifices, but

> *Let justice well up as waters,*
> *and righteousness as a mighty stream.* (Amos 5:24)

Isaiah tells us

> *The Lord of Hosts shall be exalted in justice,*
> *The Holy God shows Himself holy in righteousness.*
> (Isa. 5:16)

The prophets constantly stress the importance of applying justice:

> Learn to do well—seek justice, relieve the oppressed, judge the fatherless, plead for the widow.... Zion shall be redeemed with justice, and they that return of her with righteousness.
> Isaiah 1:17,27

To practice justice is considered among the highest demands of prophetic religion:

> *It hath been told thee, O man, what is good,*
> *And what the Lord doth require of thee:*
> *Only to do justly, love mercy*
> *And walk humbly with thy God.*
> Micah 6:8

The prophet Amos warns the people that without the practice of justice, God is repelled by their worship (5:23,24):

> *Take away from Me the noise of thy songs;*
> *And let Me not hear the melody of thy psalteries.*

But let justice well up as waters,
And righteousness as a mighty stream.

The practice of justice is even part of the symbolic betrothal between the Jewish people and God:

> And I will betroth thee unto Me forever; Yea, I will betroth thee unto Me in righteousness, justice, loving-kindness, and compassion. And I will betroth thee unto Me in faithfulness. And thou shalt know the Lord.
>
> Hosea 2:21-22

Justice is such an important concept in Judaism that the patriarch Abraham even pleads with God to practice justice: "That be far from Thee to do after this manner, to slay the righteous with the wicked,...shall not the judge of all the earth do justly?" (Genesis 18:25)

Rabbi Emanuel Rackman points out that Judaism teaches a special kind of justice, an "empathic justice," which

> ...seeks to make people identify themselves with each other—with each other's needs, with each other's hopes and aspirations, with each other's defeats and frustrations. Because Jews have known the distress of slaves and the loneliness of strangers, we are to project ourselves into their souls and make their plight our own.[22]

He points out that in 36 places in the Torah we are commanded not to mistreat the stranger in our midst.[23]

3. GIVING CHARITY (*TZEDAKAH*)

To help the poor and hungry, Judaism places great stress on the giving of charity. The Hebrew word for charity (*tzedakah*) literally means righteousness. In the Jewish tradition, *tzedakah* is not an act of condescension from one person to another who is in need. It is the fulfillment of a *mitzvah*, a commandment, to a fellow human being, who has equal status before God.

In the Jewish tradition, failure to give charity is equivalent to idolatry.[24] So important was the giving of charity by Jews that Maimonides was able to say: "Never have I seen or heard of a Jewish community that did not have a charity fund."[25]

Charity was considered so important that it took priority even over the building of the Temple. King Solomon was prohibited from using the silver and gold that David, his father, had accumulated for the building of the Temple, because that wealth should have been used to feed the poor during the three years of famine in King David's reign (1 Kings 7:51). Judaism urges lending to needy people, to help them become economically self-sufficient:

> And if thy brother be waxen poor, and his means fail with thee; then shalt thou uphold him:... Take no interest of him or increase.... Thou shalt not give him thy money upon interest....
> Leviticus 25:35-37

Every third year of the sabbatical cycle, the needy were to be recipients of the tithe for the poor (one-tenth of one's income) (Deuteronomy 14:28; 26:12).

The general Jewish view toward aiding the poor is indicated in the following verse from the Torah:

> If there be among you a needy man, one of thy brethren, within any of thy gates, in thy land which the Lord thy God giveth thee, thou shalt not harden thy heart, nor shut thy hand from thy needy brother; but thou shalt surely open thy hand unto him, and shalt surely lend him sufficient for his need in that which he wanteth.
> Deuteronomy 15:7-8

According to Maimonides, the highest form of *tzedakah* is to prevent a person from becoming poor by providing a loan, a gift, or a job so that he can adequately support himself.[26] Consistent with this concept is the following Talmudic teaching:

> It is better to lend to a poor person than to give him alms, and best of all is to provide him with capital for business.[27]

4. REDUCING POVERTY

Judaism places emphasis on charity because of the great difficulties that poor people face:

> If all afflictions in the world were assembled on one side of the scale and poverty on the other, poverty would outweigh them all.[28]

Judaism believes that poverty is destructive to the human personality and negatively shapes a person's life experiences: "The ruin of the poor is their poverty" (Prov. 10:15). "Where there is no sustenance, there is no learning."[29] "The world is darkened for him who has to look to others for sustenance."[30] "The sufferings of poverty cause a person to disregard his own sense (of right) and that of his maker."[31]

The negative effects of poverty are so severe that the Talmud makes the startling statement that "the poor person is considered as if he were dead."[32] Judaism does not encourage an ascetic life. Insufficiency of basic necessities does not ease the path toward holiness.

Many Torah laws are designed to aid the poor: the corners of the field are to be left uncut for the poor to pick (Lev. 19:9); the gleanings of the wheat harvest and fallen fruit are to be left for the poor (Lev. 19:10); during the sabbatical year, the land is to be left fallow so that the poor (as well as animals) may eat of whatever grows freely (Lev. 25:2-7).

Failure to treat the poor properly is a desecration of God: "Whoso mocketh the poor blasphemeth his maker" (Prov. 17:5). Our father Abraham always went out of his way to aid the poor. He set up inns on the highways so that the poor and the wayfarer would have access to food and drink when in need.[33]

There are several indications in the Jewish tradition that God sides with the poor and oppressed. He intervened in Egypt on behalf of poor, wretched slaves. His prophets constantly castigated those who oppressed the needy. Two proverbs reinforce this message. A negative formulation is in Proverbs 14:31: "He who oppresses a poor man insults his Maker." Proverbs 19:17 puts it more positively: "He who is kind to the poor lends to the Lord." Hence helping a needy person is like providing a loan to the Creator of the universe.

5. APPLYING COMPASSION

Closely related to the Jewish values of justice and charity is the importance the Jewish tradition places on compassion. The entire Torah is designed to teach us to be compassionate: "The purpose of the laws of the Torah is to promote compassion, loving-kindness and peace in the world."[34] The Talmud teaches that "Jews are compassionate children of compassionate parents, and one who shows no pity for fellow creatures is assuredly not of the seed of Abraham, our father."[35] The rabbis considered Jews to be distinguished by three characteristics: compassion, modesty, and benevolence.[36] As indicated previously, we are to feel empathy for strangers, "for we were strangers in the land of Egypt" (Deut. 10:19). The *bircat hamazon* (grace recited after meals) speaks of God feeding the whole world with compassion.

While in Egypt, Joseph had two sons during the seven good years of food production, but no children during the seven years of famine. The great Jewish commentator Rashi interprets this to mean that while people are starving, others who have enough should engage in acts of self-denial to show compassion and sympathy.[37]

We are not only to have concern and compassion for Jews, but for all who are in need.

> Have we not all one Father? Hath not one God created us? Why, then, do we deal treacherously with one another, profaning the covenant of our ancestors? (Mal. 2:10)

> 'Are you not like the Ethiopians to Me, O people of Israel?' says the Lord. 'Did I not bring up Israel from the land of Egypt and the Philistines from Caphtor and the Syrians from Kir?' (Amos 9:7)

As indicated previously, we are to help even our enemies when they lack sufficient food or water (Prov. 25:21).

Rabbi Hirsch writes very eloquently of the importance of compassion:

> Do not suppress this compassion, this sympathy, especially with the sufferings of your fellowman. It is the warning voice of duty, which points out to you your brother in every sufferer, and your

> own sufferings in his, and awakens the love which tells you that you belong to him and his sufferings with all the powers that you have. Do not suppress it!... See in it the admonition of God that you are to have no joy so long as a brother suffers by your side.[38]

6. SHARING

Compassion for the poor and hungry is not enough. A fundamental Jewish principle is that those who have much should share with others who are less fortunate. The Talmudic sage Hillel stresses that we must not be concerned only with our own welfare. "If I am not for myself, who will be for me? But if I am for myself alone, what am I?"[39] The *Haggadah*, which we read at the Passover seder, exhorts us to share. We are to reach out to all who are hungry and in need. The act of prolonging one's meal, on the chance that a poor person may come so that one may give him food, is so meritorious that the table of the person who does this is compared to the altar of the ancient Temple.[40]

Judaism's great emphasis on sharing is also illustrated in the following chassidic tale:

> The story is told of a great rabbi who is given the privilege of seeing the realms of Heaven and Hell before his death. He was taken first to Hell, where he was confronted with a huge banquet room in the middle of which was a large elegant table covered with a magnificent white tablecloth, the finest china, silver, and crystal. The table was covered from one end to the other with the most delicious foods that the eyes have ever seen or the mouth tasted. And all around the table people were sitting looking at the food...and wailing.
>
> It was such a wail that the rabbi had never heard such a sad sound in his entire life and he asked, "With a luxurious table and the most delicious food, why do these people wail so bitterly?" As he entered the room, he saw the reason for their distress. For although each was confronted with this incredible sight before him, no one was able to eat the food. Each person's arms were splinted so that the elbows could not bend. They could touch the food but could not eat it. The anguish this caused was the reason for the great wail and despair that the rabbi saw and heard.

> He was next shown Heaven, and to his surprise he was confronted by the identical scene witnessed in Hell: The large banquet room, elegant table, lavish settings, and sumptuous foods. And, in addition, once again everyone's arms were splinted so the elbows could not bend. Here, however, there was no wailing, but rather joy greater than he had ever experienced in his life. For whereas here too the people could not put the food into their own mouths, each picked up the food and fed it to another. They were thus able to enjoy, not only the beautiful scene, the wonderful smells, and the delicious foods, but the joy of sharing and helping one another.[41]

Rabbi Jay Marcus of the Young Israel of Staten Island commented on the fact that *karpas* (eating of greens) and *yahatz* (breaking of the middle matzah for later use as the dessert) are next to each other in the Passover seder service.[42] Those who can live on simple things like greens (vegetables, etc.) will most readily divide their possessions and share with others.

To help share God's abundant harvests with the poor, the Torah instructs farmers:

> 1) If less than three ears of corn were dropped during the harvest, they were not to be gleaned, but were to be left for the poor (*Leket*).
> 2) A sheaf forgotten by the farmer could not be retrieved but had to be left for the poor (*Shik'khah*).
> 3) A corner of the field always had to be left unharvested; it was the property of the poor (*Pe'ah*).
> 4) Every third year a part of the tithe of the harvest had to be set aside for the poor (*Ma'aser Ani*).
> 5) On the eve of every holy day, "*mat'not Yad*," a special gift to the poor, had to be put aside.

Vegetarianism is consistent with this Jewish concept of sharing. As Jay Dinshah, former president of the North American Vegetarian Society, states:

> After all, vegetarianism is, more than anything else, the very essence and the very expression of altruistic SHARING,... the

> sharing of the One Life,... the sharing of the natural resources of the Earth,... the sharing of love, kindness, compassion, and beauty in this life.[43]

Recently a new Jewish group, Mazon, was formed to help Jews share their joyous events with hungry people. It urges people to contribute 3 percent of the money spent for weddings, bar mitzvahs, and other celebrations to the group which funnels the money to organizations working to reduce hunger. Its address is Mazon, 2288 Westwood Blvd., Los Angeles, CA 90024.

7. SIMPLIFYING LIFE STYLES

While millions starve, it is imperative that those who have much simplify their lives so they can share more with others.

A group of outstanding religious leaders, including representatives of different branches of Judaism in the United States and Israel, met in Bellagio, Italy, in May 1975 to consider "The Energy/Food Crisis: A Challenge to Peace, a Call to Faith." They agreed on a statement that included this assertion:

> The deepest and strongest expression of any religion is the 'styles of life' that characterizes its believers. It is urgent that religious communities and individuals scrutinize their life style and turn from habits of waste, overconsumption, and thoughtless acceptance of the standards propagated by advertisements and social pressures.
>
> The cry from millions for food brought us together from many faiths. God—Reality itself—calls us to respond to the cry for food. And we hear it as a cry not only for aid but also for justice.[44]

Simpler life styles, with less wasteful diets, can be an important first step toward justice for the hungry of the world. Simpler diets do not imply a lack of joy or a lack of fellowship. As Proverbs 15:17 states: "Better a dinner of herbs where love is than a stalled ox with hatred."

During the Middle Ages, local Jewish councils sometimes set up "sumptuary laws" for the community; people were forbidden to spend more than a limited amount of money at weddings and other occasions.

These laws were designed so that the poor should not be embarrassed at not being able to match the expenditures of the wealthy and so that a financial strain was not placed on the community as a whole. Perhaps the spirit of such laws should be invoked today. Can we continue to consume flesh that wastes so much grain at a time when many are starving? Is it not now time for officiating rabbis to specify guidelines to reduce waste and ostentation at weddings, bar mitzvahs, and other occasions?

SUMMARY

Can a shift to vegetarian diets make a difference with regard to world hunger? Consider these statistics:

(1) Two hundred and twenty million Americans are eating enough food (largely because of the high consumption of grain-fed livestock) to feed over 1 billion people in the poor countries.[45]

(2) The world's cattle consume an amount of food equivalent to the calorie requirements of 8.7 billion people.[46] Livestock in the U. S. consume ten times the grain that Americans eat directly.[47]

(3) Harvard nutritionist Jean Mayer estimates that if people reduced their meat consumption by just 10 percent, enough grain would be released to feed 60 million people.[48]

(4) The wealthy nations feed more grain to their livestock than the people of India and China (more than one-third of the human race) consume directly.[49]

(5) Contrary to the common belief that our grain exports help feed a hungry world, two-thirds of our agricultural exports go to feed livestock[50], rather than hungry people.

These facts indicate that the food being fed to animals in the affluent nations could, if properly distributed, end both hunger and malnutrition throughout the world. A switch from flesh-centered diets would free land and other resources, which could be used to grow nutritious crops for people. It would then be necessary to promote policies that would enable people in the underdeveloped countries to use their resources and skills to become food self-reliant.

Two quotations reinforce these conclusions: Mahatma Gandhi stated: "There is enough for the world's need but not for its greed." Sister Elizabeth Seton asserted that we should "live simply, that others may simply live."

With so much hunger, poverty, and injustice in the world, explicit Jewish mandates to feed the hungry, help the poor, share resources, practice charity, show compassion, and pursue justice, and the trials and tribulations of Jewish history point to vegetarianism as the diet most consistent with Jewish values.

5

Judaism, Vegetarianism, and Ecology

The earth is the Lord's and the fullness thereof. (Psalm 24:1)

JUDAISM ON ECOLOGY

Many fundamental Torah principles are related to the above statement:

(1) People are to be co-workers with God in helping to preserve and improve the world.

The Talmudic sages assert that people's role is to enhance the world as "co-partners of God in the work of creation."[1] There is a *Midrash* (a story that teaches a Torah lesson based on biblical events and values) that beautifully expresses the idea that God needs people to help tend the world:

> In the hour when the Holy one, blessed be He,
> created the first man,
> He took him and let him pass before all the trees of
> the Garden of Eden and said to him:
> "See my works, how fine and excellent they are!
> Now all that I have created, for you have I created.
> Think upon this and do not corrupt and desolate My World,
> For if you corrupt it, there is no one to set it
> right after you."[2]

The Psalmist also expresses the idea that God the Creator treats every person as a partner in the work of creation (Psalm 8:4-7):

> When I look at Your heavens, the work of Your hands,
> The moon and work which you have established,
> What is man that You are mindful of him, and the son of man that You do care for him?
> Yet you have made him little less than God, and do crown him with glory and honor.
> You have given him dominion over the works of Your hands;
> You have put all things under his feet....

The talmudic sages indicate great concern about preserving the environment and preventing pollution. They state: "It is forbidden to live in a town which has no garden or greenery."[3] Threshing floors had to be placed far enough from a town so that it would not be dirtied by chaff carried by winds.[4] Tanneries had to be kept at least 50 cubits from a town and could be placed only on the east side of a town, so that odors would not be carried by the prevailing winds from the west.[5] The rabbis express a sense of sanctity toward the environment: "the atmosphere (air) of the land of Israel makes one wise."[6]

(2) Everything belongs to God. We are to be stewards of the earth, to see that its produce is available for all God's children.

There is an apparent contradiction between two verses in Psalms: "The earth is the Lord's" (Ps. 24:1) and "The heavens are the heavens of God, but the earth He has given to the children of man" (Ps. 115:16). The apparent discrepancy is cleared up in the following way: Before a person says a *b'racha* (a blessing), before he acknowledges God's ownership of the land and its products, then "the earth is the Lord's"; after a person has said a *b'racha*, acknowledging God's ownership and that we are stewards to see that God's works are properly used and shared, ***then*** "the earth He has given to the children of man."[7]

Property is a sacred trust given by God; it must be used to fulfill God's purposes. No person has absolute or exclusive control over his or her possessions. The concept that people have custodial care of the earth, as opposed to ownership, is illustrated by this story from the Talmud:

> Two men were fighting over a piece of land. Each claimed ownership and bolstered his claim with apparent proof. To resolve their differences, they agreed to put the case before the rabbi. The rabbi listened but could come to no decision because both seemed to be right. Finally he said, "Since I cannot decide to whom this land belongs, let us ask the land." He put his ear to the ground and, after a moment, straightened up. "Gentlemen, the land says it belongs to neither of you but that you belong to it."[8]

As indicated previously, even the produce of the field does not belong solely to the person who farms the land. The poor are entitled to a portion:

> And when ye reap the harvest of your land, thou shalt not wholly reap the corner of thy field, neither shalt thou gather the gleaning of thy harvest. And thou shalt not glean thy vineyard, neither shalt thou gather the fallen fruit of thy vineyard; thou shalt leave them for the poor and for the stranger; I am the Lord, thy God. (Lev. 19:9-10)

These portions set aside for the poor were not voluntary contributions based on kindness. They were, in essence, a regular divine assessment. Because God was the real owner of the land, he claimed a share of His own gifts for the poor.

As a reminder that "the earth is the Lord's," the land must be permitted to rest and lie fallow every seven years (the sabbatical year):

> And six years thou shalt sow thy land, and gather in the increase thereof, but the seventh year thou shalt let it rest and lay fallow, that the poor of thy people may eat; and what they leave, the beast of the field shall eat. In like manner thou shalt deal with the vineyard, and with thy oliveyard. (Exod. 23:10-11)

The sabbatical year also has ecological benefits. The land was given a chance to rest and renew its fertility.

Judaism asserts that there is one God who created the entire earth as a unity, in ecological balance, and that everything is connected to everything else. This idea is perhaps best expressed by Psalm 104:

> ...Thou [God] art the One Who sends forth springs into
> brooks, that they may run between mountains,
> To give drink to every beast of the fields; the creatures
> of the forest quench their thirst.
> Beside them dwell the fowl of the heavens;...
> Thou art He Who waters the mountains from His upper
> chambers;...
> Thou art He Who causes the grass to spring up for the
> cattle and herb, for the service of man, to bring forth
> bread from the earth....
> How manifold art Thy works, O Lord! In wisdom hast Thou
> made them all; the earth is full of Thy property....

(3) We are not to waste or destroy unnecessarily anything of value.

This prohibition, called *bal tashchit* ("thou shalt not destroy") is based on the following Torah statement:

> When thou shalt besiege a city a long time, in making war against it to take it, thou shall not destroy (*lo tashchit*) the trees thereof by wielding an ax against them; for thou mayest eat of them but thou shalt not cut them down; for is the tree of the field man, that it should be besieged of thee? Only the trees of which thou knoweth that they are not trees for food, them thou mayest destroy and cut down, that thou mayest build bulwarks against the city that maketh war with thee, until it fall. (Deut. 20:19-20)

This prohibition against destroying fruit-bearing trees in time of warfare was extended by the Jewish sages. It it forbidden to cut down even a barren tree or to waste anything if no useful purpose is accomplished.[9] The sages of the Talmud made a general prohibition against waste: "Whoever breaks vessels or tears garments, or destroys a building, or clogs up a fountain, or destroys food violates the prohibition of *bal tashchit*."[10] In summary, *bal tashchit* prohibits the destruction, complete or incomplete, direct or indirect, of all objects of potential benefit to people.

The seriousness with which the rabbis considered the violation of *bal tashchit* is illustrated by the following talmudic statements:

> The sage Rabbi Hanina attributed the early death of his son to the fact that the boy had chopped down a fig tree.[11]
>
> Jews should be taught when very young that it is a sin to waste even small amounts of food.[12]
>
> Rav Zutra taught: "One who covers an oil lamp or uncovers a naptha lamp transgresses the prohibition of *bal tashchit*"[13] Each action mentioned would cause a faster (hence wasteful) consumption of the fuel.

Rabbi Samson Raphael Hirsch states that *bal tashchit* is the first and most general call of God: We are to "regard things as God's property and use them with a sense of responsibility for wise human purposes. Destroy nothing! Waste nothing!"[14] He states that destruction includes using more things (or things of greater value) than is necessary to obtain one's aim.[15] The following *midrash* is related to this concept:

> Two men entered a shop. One ate coarse bread and vegetables, while the other ate fine bread, fat meat, and drank old wine. The one who ate fine food suffered harm, while the one who had coarse food escaped harm. Observe how simply animals live and how healthy they are as a result.[16]

ECOLOGY IN JEWISH HISTORY AND PRAYERS

Much of early Jewish history is closely related to the natural environment. The patriarchs and their descendants were shepherds. Their work led them into many types of natural settings, including mountains, prairies, wilderness, and desert. They thus developed a love and appreciation of natural wonders and beauty. According to Charles W. Eliot, "no race has ever surpassed the Jewish descriptions of either the beauties or the terrors of the nature which environs man."[17]

The greatest prophet, Moses, while a shepherd, learned many facts about nature which were useful in leading the Israelites in the desert. The Ten Commandments and the Torah were revealed to the Jews at Mount Sinai, in a natural setting. The forty years of wandering in the wilderness trained Israel in the appreciation of natural beauty.

Jews have often pictured God through His handiwork in nature. Abraham, the father of the Jewish people, when marveling at the heavenly bodies, intuited that there must be a creator of these wonders. The prophet Isaiah stated:

> Lift up thine eyes on high,
> And see: Who hath created these?
> He that bringeth out their host by numbers,
> He calleth them all by name;
> By the greatness of His might, for He is strong in power,
> Not one faileth.
>
> Isaiah 40:26

Many Jewish prayers extol God for His wondrous creations. In the morning, religious Jews say the following prayer to thank God for the new day:

> Blessed art Thou, O Lord our God, King of the universe.
> Who formest light and createst darkness,
> Who makest peace and createst all things.
> Who in mercy givest light to the earth
> And to them that dwell thereon,
> And in Thy goodness renewest the creation
> Every day continually.
> How manifold are Thy works, O Lord!
> In wisdom hast Thou made them all;
> The earth is full of Thy possessions....
> Be Thou blessed, O Lord our God,
> For the excellency of Thy handiwork,
> And for the bright luminaries
> Which Thou hast made:
> They shall glorify Thee forever.

At the Sabbath morning services, the following prayer is recited: "The heavens declare the glory of God, and the firmament showest His handiwork" (Psalms 19:2).

The sensitivity of the Torah to environmental cleanliness is illustrated by the following law, which commands disposal of sewage, even in wartime, by burial in the ground, not by dumping into rivers or littering the countryside!

> Thou shalt have a place outside the military camp, whither thou shalt go forth abroad. And thou shalt have a spade among thy weapons; and it shalt be when thou sittest down outside, thou shalt dig therewith, and shalt turn back and cover that which cometh from thee.
>
> Deuteronomy 23:13-15

The preservation of the land of Israel has been a central theme in Judaism. The three festivals (Pesach, Shavuot, and Sukkot) are agricultural as well as spiritual celebrations. Jews pray for dew and rain in their proper time so that there will be abundant harvests in Israel. Jewish tradition militates against abuse of natural resources and the environment.

ECOLOGICAL PROBLEMS RELATED TO CURRENT LIVESTOCK AGRICULTURE

Unfortunately, the wisdom of *bal tashchit* is seldom applied today. Our society is based on waste, on buying, using, and throwing away. Advertisements constantly try to make us feel guilty if we do not have the newest gadgets and the latest styles of clothing. Every national holiday in the United States has become an orgy of consumption.

Our flesh-centered diets are extremely wasteful:

(1) The average person in the United States eats almost five times as much grain (mostly in the form of animal products) as does a person in an undeveloped country.[18]

(2) It takes 16 pounds of grain and soybeans to produce one pound of beef on our plates in the United States. For livestock in general, it takes 7 pounds of grain and soybeans for that one pound of beef.[19] For comparison purposes, 16 pounds of grain have 21 times more calories and 8 times more protein (but only 3 times more fat) than a pound of hamburger.[20]

(3) Over 80% of the grain grown in the United States is fed to animals.[21] Perhaps the modern counterpart of destroying fruit-bearing trees is taking grains which could feed starving people and feeding them to animals.

(4) Half of our harvested acreage is devoted to feed-crops.[22]

(5) A nonvegetarian diet requires about 3.5 acres/person, whereas a total vegetarian (vegan) diet requires only about a fifth of an acre.[23] Hence, a shift to vegetarian diets would free much valuable land, which could be used to grow nutritious crops for people.

(6) The standard diet of a person in the United States requires 4,200 gal. of water/day (for animals' drinking water, irrigation of crops, processing, washing, cooking, etc.)[24] A person on a pure vegetarian diet requires as little as 300 gal./day.[25]

The production of only one pound of steak uses 2,500 gallons of water. Livestock production consumes over 80% of all the water used in the U.S., and this water is becoming increasingly scarce.[26] Studies have indicated that if the entire U.S. population were total vegetarians, no irrigation water at all would be needed to produce our food.[27] *Newsweek* recently reported that "the water that goes into a 1,000 pound steer would float a destroyer."[28]

(7) A nonvegetarian diet also wastes much energy. In the United States, an average of 10 calories of fuel energy are required for every calorie of food energy obtained; in many other countries, they gain 20 or more calories of food energy per calorie of fuel energy.[29] To produce one pound of steak (500 calories of food energy) requires 20,000 calories of fossil fuels, most of which is expended for feed-crops.[30] It requires 78 calories of fossil fuel for each calorie of protein obtained from feedlot produced beef.[31] Grains and beans require only two to five percent as much fossil fuel.[32] Energy input to the U.S. food system now accounts for about 16.5% of the total energy budget.[33]

(8) According to a comprehensive study sponsored by the U.S. Departments of Interior and Commerce, the value of raw materials consumed to produce food from livestock is greater than the value of all oil, gas, and coal produced in this country.[34] A third of the value of all raw materials consumed in the U.S. for *all* purposes is consumed in livestock foods.[35]

As these facts indicate, a vegetarian diet is far less wasteful than a meat-centered diet and is therefore much more consistent with the principle of *bal tashchit.*

Modern agricultural methods related to meat production are a prime cause of the environmental crises facing the United States and much of the world today.

(1) The tremendous quantity of grains grown to feed animals requires extensive use of chemical fertilizer and pesticides. Much air and water pollution is caused by the production and use of these products. Various constituents of fertilizer, particularly nitrogen, are washed into surface waters. High levels of nitrates in drinking water have caused illnesses for people as well as animals.[36]

(2) Mountains of manure produced by cattle raised in feedlots wash into and pollute streams, rivers, and underground water sources. American livestock produce about 2 billion tons of waste annually[37]—more than ten times that produced by human, and equivalent to the waste of nearly half the world's human population.[38] Food geographer, Georg Borgstrom has estimated that American livestock contribute five times more organic waste to water pollution than do people, and twice as much as industry.[39]

(3) The production of feed-crops for animals is "mining" our soil. Each year over 5 billion tons of topsoil are eroded in the U.S., almost all due to livestock agriculture.[40] In some places, erosion is as bad or worse than during the Dust Bowl period.[41] William Brune, Iowa state conservation official in 1976, warned that two bushels of topsoil are being lost for every bushel of corn

harvested in Iowa's sloping soils.[42] In some areas lower yields are occurring due to erosion and the reduction in fertility that it causes.[43]

(4) Large areas of land throughout the world have been destroyed by grazing animals. Overgrazing has been a prime cause of erosion in various parts of the world throughout history. Over 60 percent of all U.S. rangelands are overgrazed, with billions of tons of soil lost every year.[44]

(5) The huge amounts of grain grown to feed animals require increasing amounts of pesticides. While the amount of DDT is going down since it was banned for use in the U.S. in 1972, our intake of other dangerous pesticides like malathion, toxaphene, and captan, is increasing.[45] Also, in a "circle of poison", pesticides banned or heavily restricted in the U.S. are legally exported to poor countries where they have been used on foods imported into the United States. Dangers to health due to the biological magnification of pesticides in the body fat of animals have been previously discussed.

(6) Slaughterhouses are also prime sources of pollution. One study revealed that 18 meat-packing companies in Omaha, Nebraska, discharge over 100,000 pounds of grease, carcass dressing, carcass cleaning, intestinal waste, paunch manure, and fecal matter from viscera into the sewer system that empties into the Missouri River.[46]

(7) Demand for meat in wealthy countries also leads to environmental damage in poor countries. To save 5 cents on a fast-food hamburger exported to the U.S., the earth's tropical rain forests are being bulldozed at a rate of 100 acres per minute, a rate which would destroy an area the size of Pennsylvania every year.[47] Each fast-food hamburger patty requires the destruction of 55 square feet of tropical forest for grazing.[48] Half are already gone forever, and at current rates of destruction, the rest will be gone by the middle of the next century. What makes this especially serious is that half of the world's species of plants and animals

> reside in tropical rain forests, and some might hold secrets for cures of some of today's deadly diseases. Also, reduced rain forests would alter climate and reduce rainfall with potentially devastating effects on the world's agriculture.

When we consider all of these negative environmental factors, and then add the very harmful effects related to human health and global hunger, we can safely assert that, next to the threat of nuclear war, flesh-centered diets and the livestock agriculture needed to sustain it are the greatest threats to global survival today. Also, while hopefully nuclear war will never occur, the negative effects of meat-based agriculture occur daily.

CONCLUSION

Vegetarianism relates to a simplification of agricultural practices which would put far less stress on the environment. Land presently used to grow feed-crops could be used to raise food for hungry people and to lay fallow periodically, thus enabling it to improve its productivity. Far less chemical fertilizer and pesticides would be necessary. There would be far less demand on scarce water, fuel, and other resources. Giant feed lots, which result in much animal manure washing into streams and rivers, could be converted to more ecologically sound uses.

Contrary to the ecological benefits of the sabbatical year, the fertility of cleared soil has been greatly reduced in recent years by overuse and heavy utilization of chemical fertilizers and pesticides. Philip Pick, editor of the Jewish Vegetarian, points out that only under a vegetarian economy can the sabbatical year be observed today:

> It [the sabbatical year] does not provide for shiploads of fodder to be removed from the land and exported to feed factory farm birds and beasts incarcerated....The wastages would be too great; over ninety percent of this produce is lost in conversion to flesh, and the undernourished people in the grain growing countries would suffer still further by the denial of the Sabbath produce of their land. Indeed the present system of factory farming would not be possible if the Sabbatical were recognized.[49]

The sabbatical year provided for beasts of the field to eat from that which would grow freely on farms, vineyards, and oliveyards. What a tremendous difference this is from current practices of chemical feeding of animals in darkened cells where they spend all their wretched lives.

The concept of the sabbatical year is one answer to people's problems today. Consider one year without tremendous amounts of chemicals and fertilizers that pollute our air and water and reduce the fertility of the soil. Consider the benefits to people of getting away for a year from their lives of hustle and bustle, the shrieking of the marketplace, and the constant need to amass more and more goods; instead there could be a utilization of time for mental and spiritual development and perhaps a study of methods of reducing economic and military disputes.

The aims of vegetarians and ecologists are similar: simplify our life styles, have regard for the earth and all forms of life, and hence apply the knowledge that "the earth is the Lord's."

6

Judaism, Vegetarianism, and Peace

> World peace, or any other kind of peace, depends greatly on the attitude of the mind. Vegetarianism can bring about the right mental attitude for peace. In this world of lusts and hatred, greed and anger, force and violence, vegetarianism holds forth a way of life which, if practiced universally, can lead to a better, juster, and more peaceful community of nations.
>
> U Nu, former prime minister of Burma

Our age is continuously threatened by violence, war, and the threat of war. Jewish teachings related to peace and vegetarianism can reduce the potential for violence and war.

JEWISH TEACHINGS ON PEACE

The Jewish tradition mandates a special obligation to work for peace. The Bible does not command that people merely love peace or merely seek peace but that they actively pursue peace. The rabbis of the Talmud state that there are many commandments that require a certain time and place for their performance, but with regard to peace, "seek peace and pursue it" (Ps. 34:15); you are to seek it in your own place and pursue it everywhere else.[1] The famous Talmudic sage, Hillel, states that we should "be of the disciples of Aaron, loving peace and pursuing peace."[2]

On the special duty of Jews to work for peace, the sages comment: "Said the Holy one blessed be He: The whole Torah is peace and to whom do I give it? To the nation which loves peace!"[3]

The rabbis of the Talmud used lavish words of praise to indicate the significance of peace:

> Great is peace, for God's name is peace.... Great is peace, for it encompasses all blessings.... Great is peace, for even in times of war, peace must be sought.... Great is peace seeing that when the Messiah is to come, He will commence with peace, as it is said, "How beautiful upon the mountains are the feet of the messenger of good tidings, who announces peace" (Isa. 52:7).[4]

> The whole Torah was given for the sake of peace, and it is said, "all her paths are peace" (Prov. 3:17).[5]

The important Jewish prayers, such as the *Amidah* (*Sh'moneh Esrei*), the kaddish, the priestly blessing, and the grace after meals, all conclude with a prayer for peace.

In spite of Judaism's historical aversion to idolotry, peace is so important that the rabbis taught:

> If Israel should worship idols, but she be at peace, God had no power, in effect, over them.[6]

The Jewish tradition does not mandate absolute pacifism, or peace at any price. The Israelites often went forth to battle and not always in defensive wars. But they always held to the ideal of universal peace and yearned for the day when there would be no more bloodshed or violence:

> *And they shall beat their swords into plowshares,*
> *And their spears into pruning hooks;*
> *Nation shall not lift up sword against nation,*
> *Neither shall they learn war any more.*
> *But they shall sit every man under his vine and*
> *under his fig tree;*
> *And none shall make them afraid;*
> *For the mouth of the Lord of hosts has spoken.*
> (Mic. 4:3-4; Isa. 2:4)

Judaism teaches that violence and war result directly from injustice:

> The sword comes into the world because of justice delayed, because of justice perverted, and because of those who render wrong decisions.[7]

The Hebrew word for war, *milchama*, is directly derived from the word locham, which means both "to feed" as well as "to wage war."[8] The Hebrew word for bread, *lechem*, comes from the same root. This led the sages to suggest that lack of bread and the search for sufficient food tempt people to make war. The seeds of war are often found in the inability of a nation to provide adequate food for its people. Hence, feeding the tremendous amounts of grains to animals destined for slaughter, instead of feeding starving people, is a prime cause for war.

LINKS BETWEEN FLESH-CENTERED DIETS AND VIOLENCE AMONG PEOPLE

1. Views of Jewish Sages and Prophets

Many Jewish sages felt that the biblical laws related to kindness to animals were meant to condition people to be considerate of fellow human beings. Several medieval Jewish philosophers including R. Isaac Abarbanel (1437-1509) and R. Joseph Albo consider vegetarianism to be a moral ideal because it avoids the meanness and cruelty associated with meat consumption and the harsh treatment of animals.[9]

Commenting on the biblical prohibition against taking a mother bird with her young, Nachmanides states:

> The motivating purpose is to teach us the quality of compassion and not to become cruel; for cruelty expands in a man's soul, as is well known with respect to cattle slaughterers...[10]

Maimonides indicates that the general obligation with regard to *tsa'ar ba'alei chayim*

> is set down with a view to protecting us that we not acquire moral habits of cruelty and learn to inflict pain gratuitously, but that we should be kind and merciful...[11]

The *Sefer Hachinuch* connects the muzzling of an ox treading corn to the negative treatment of human laborers:

> When a man becomes accustomed to have pity even upon animals who were created to serve us, and he gives them a portion of their labors, his soul will likewise grow accustomed to be kind to human beings...[12]

Abraham Ibn Ezra, Abarbanel and Moses Luzzato (1707-1747) taught that boiling a kid in its mother's milk was a barbaric practice that could lead people to cruel acts.[13]

Rabbi Samson Raphael Hirsch stresses that vegetables are the preferable food to help make the human body an instrument of the soul and to implement its aims of holiness and moral freedom.[14] He indicated that every food which makes the body too active in a carnal direction makes people more indifferent and less sensitive to the loftier impulses of the moral life.[15] He also states, "The boy who, in crude joy, finds delight in the convulsions of an injured beetle or the anxiety of a suffering animal will soon also be dumb toward human pain."[16]

The prophet Isaiah (66:3) states, "He who kills an ox is as if he slew a person." There are several ways of interpreting this verse from a vegetarian point of view:

(1) By eating animals, we are consuming the grain that fattened the animal; this grain could have been used to save human lives.

(2) In poor countries, the ox helps farmers to plow the earth and grow food. Hence the killing of an ox leads to less production of food and hence more starvation.

(3) When a person is ready to kill an animal for his pleasure or profit, he may be more ready to kill another human being.

2. OTHER VIEWS

Many people relate the cruelty involved in slaughtering animals for food to cruelty to people and eventually to war.

G. S. Arundale, late president of the Theosophic Society, discussed the relationship between the treatment of animals and war:

> Whenever I see a meat and fish-ridden dining table, I know that I am looking upon one of the seeds of war and hatred—a seed that develops into an ugly weed of atrocity.... When people ask me, "Is there likely to be a future war?" I answer, "Yes, until the animals are treated as our younger brothers."[17]

Albert Einstein stated:

> The vegetarian manner of living, by its purely physical effect on the human temperament, would most beneficially influence the lot of mankind.[18]

The relationship between the consumption of meat and war is dramatized by the following dialogue from Plato's *Republic*:

> *...and there will be animals of many other kinds,*
> *if people eat them?*
> *Certainly.*
> *And living in this way we shall have much greater*
> *need of physicians than before?*
> *Much greater.*
> *And the country which was enough to support the*
> *original inhabitants will be too small now, and*
> *not enough?*
> *Quite true.*
> *Then a slice of our neighbors' land will be wanted*
> *by us for pasture and tillage, and they will want a*
> *slice of ours, if, like ourselves, they exceed the*
> *limit of necessity, and give themselves up to the*
> *unlimited accumulation of wealth?*
> *That, Socrates, will be inevitable.*
> *And so, we shall go to war, Glaucon. Shall we not?*
> *Most certainly, he replied.*[19]

As the following poem, *Song of Peace*, indicates, the vegetarian writer George Bernard Shaw felt that the killing of animals today logically leads to the killing of men on the battlefield tomorrow:

> *We are the living graves of murdered beasts,*
> *Slaughtered to satisfy our appetites,*
> *We never pause to wonder at our feasts,*
> *If animals like men, can possible have rights.*
> *We pray on Sundays that we may have light,*
> *To guide our foot-steps on the paths we tread,*
> *We're sick of war, we do not want to fight,*
> *The thought of it now fills our heart with dread,*
> *And yet we gorge ourselves upon the dead.*
> *Like carrion crows, we live and feed on meat,*
> *Regardless of the suffering and pain*
> *We cause by doing so. If thus we treat*
> *Defenseless animals, for sport or gain,*
> *How can we hope in this world to attain*
> *The PEACE we say we are so anxious for?*
> *We pray for it, o'er hecatombs of slain,*
> *To God, while outraging the moral law,*
> *Thus cruelty begets its offspring—War.*[20]

CONCLUSION

In view of the enormous waste of grain and other resources related to livestock agriculture, the following statement by Senator Mark Hatfield of Oregon is relevant:

> Hunger and famine will do more to destabilize this world; [they are] more explosive than all atomic weaponry possessed by the big powers. Desperate people do desperate things....Nuclear fission is now in the hands of even the developing countries in many of which hunger and famine are most serious.[21]

Richard J. Barnet, a director of the Washington-based Institute for Policy Studies and author of The Lean Years, an analysis of resource scarcities, believes that by the end of the century the anger and despair of hungry people could lead to acts of terrorism and economic class wars.[22]

Just as scarcity of food can lead to war, so can scarcity of sources of energy. A prime current threat to peace is the necessity of affluent countries to obtain sufficient oil to keep their economies running smoothly. The Persian Gulf area, where much of the world's oil is produced, is a place where recently there has been much instability and competition among the superpowers, which could result in war.

Meat-centered diets contribute to the energy crisis. It takes nearly 10 calories of fossil fuel energy to produce 1 calorie of food energy in the average American diet.[23] The main contributors to this are feedlot cattle raising and deep-sea fishing, which are very energy-intensive. It takes about 77 calories of fossil fuel energy to put 1 meat calorie on the plate.[24]

Feeding people rather than factory-bred animals requires far less irrigation, fertilizer, pesticides, mechanization, refrigeration, and processing, all of which consume much energy. The tremendous effects that meat-centered diets have on energy consumption can be seen in this example: if all the petroleum reserves in the world were devoted solely to feeding a typical North American diet to the world's more than 4 billion people, all the world's oil would be used in only 13 years.[25]

Judaism emphasizes the pursuit of justice and harmonious relations between nations to reduce violence and the prospects for war. The Prophet Isaiah states:

> And the work of righteousness shall be peace; And the effect of righteousness quietness and confidence forever. (Isa. 32:17)

The Psalmist writes,

> When loving-kindness and truth have met together, then righteousness and peace have kissed each other. (Ps. 85:11)

By adopting a diet that shows concern and loving-kindness for the hungry people of the world, by working for righteousness through more equitable sharing of God's abundant harvests, Jews and other people can play a significant role in moving the world toward that day when "nations shall not learn war any more."

7

Questions and Answers

I keep six honest serving men,
They taught me all I knew;
Their names are what and why and when,
And where and how and who.

Rudyard Kipling

Question 1. Don't Jews have to eat meat on the Sabbath and Jewish holidays?

Answer. Rabbi Yehudah, the son of Bathyra, one of the outstanding sages of the talmudic period, states that the obligation to eat meat for rejoicing applied only at the time when the Temple was in existence.[1] He adds that after the destruction of the Temple, one should rejoice with wine. Based on this, Rabbi Yishmael states, "From the day that the Holy Temple was destroyed, it would have been right to have imposed upon ourselves a law prohibiting the eating of flesh."[2] The reason that the rabbis did not make such a law was that they felt that regulations should not be imposed that the community is not ready to accept.[3] (It was also thought that meat was necessary for proper nutrition.)

Other sources who maintain that there no longer exists an obligation to partake of meat on festivals are Ritva, *Kiddushin* 36 and *Teshuvot Rashbash*, No. 176.[4] As indicated later (question 22), there are also scholars who assert that the eating of meat was not an absolute requirement even during the Temple period.

In a scholarly article in *The Journal of Halacha and Contemporary Society*, Rabbi Alfred Cohen, editor of the journal and spirital leader of the Young Israel of Canarsie, concludes that "If a person is more comfortable not eating meat, there would be no obligation for him to do so on the Sabbath" and "... we may clearly infer that eating meat, even on a Festival, is not mandated by the halacha."[5] He also points out that..."the *Shulchan Aruch* (of Beit Yosef), which is the foundation for normative law for Jews today, does not insist upon the necessity to eat meat as *simchat Yom Tov* (making the holiday joyful)".[6]

In a *responsum* (an answer to a question based on Jewish law), Rabbi Moshe Halevi Steinberg of Kiryat Yam, Israel, states, "One whose soul rebels against eating living things can without any doubt fulfill the commandment of enhancing the Sabbath and rejoicing on festivals by eating vegetarian foods... Each person should delight in the Sabbath according to his own sensibility, enjoyment, and outlook.[7] In the same *responsum*, R. Steinberg points out that there is no barrier or impediment to converting a non-Jew who is a vegetarian, since vegetarianism in no sense contradicts Jewish law.

Eating meat is a distress and torment to those who loathe it. Such people would suffer by eating flesh on the Sabbath and holy days.

Could sensitive, compassionate people enhance a joyous occasion by eating meat if they were fully aware that, for their pleasure, animals are cruelly treated, grains are fed to animals while millions of people starve, and their health is being impaired?

Question 2. If Jews don't eat meat, they'll be deprived of the opportunity to do many *mitzvot* (commandments). If God did not want meat to be eaten, why did he give so many laws concerning the slaughter, preparation, and consumption of meat?

Answer. As indicated previously, Rabbi Kook states that God provided many laws and regulations related to meat as a reproof, as a reminder that animals' lives are being destroyed, and in the hope that this would eventually lead people to vegetarianism.[8] He and others say that vegetarianism is the Jewish ideal diet and that God permitted meat eating as a concession, with many regulations designed to keep alive a sense of reverence for life.

There are other cases where laws were provided to regulate activities that God would prefer people not to do. For example, God wishes people to live at peace, but He provides commandments related to war, because he knows that human beings tend to quarrel and seek victories over others. Similarly, the laws in the Torah related to slavery are a concession to human weakness. We cannot conclude from this that we are therefore obligated to make war or own slaves. In the same way, the laws related to meat consumption don't mean that we must eat meat.

By not eating meat, Jews are directly or indirectly acting consistently with many *mitzvot* and Jewish concepts, such as showing compassion to animals, preserving health, not wasting, feeding the hungry, and preserving the earth. Also, by not eating meat, a Jew cannot violate many possible prohibitions of the Torah, such as mixing meat and milk, eating nonkosher animals, and eating blood or fat.

It should be noted that the laws of kashrut involve not only the technical details of preparing food, but also the blessings to be recited before and after eating. None of these blessings would cease with a vegetarian diet since the blessing for meat is the same as for several other foods, such as soup and juice. Also, vegetarianism would not affect "food orientated" *mitzvot* such as *kiddush*, *bircat hamazon* (blessing after meals), or Passover *seder* observances.

Question 3. Judaism considers it an *averah* (sin) not to take advantage of the pleasurable things that God has put on the earth. As he put animals on the earth and it is pleasurable to eat them, is it not an *averah* to refrain from eating meat?

Answer. Can eating meat be pleasurable to a religious person when he or she knows that as a result health is endangered, grain is wasted, and animals are being treated cruelly? There are many other ways to have pleasure without doing harm to living creatures. The prohibition against abstaining from pleasurable things only applies when there is no plausible basis for the abstention; in the case of vegetarians, they abstain because of a feeling that eating meat is injurious to health, because their soul rebels at eating a living creature, or because they wish to have a diet that minimizes threats to the environment and the use of the earth's resources.

There are other cases in Judaism where pleasurable acts are forbidden or discouraged, such as the use of tobacco, drinking liquor to excess, and sexual relations out of wedlock.

Question 4. Weren't people given dominion over animals? Didn't God put them here for our use?

Answer. Dominion does not mean that we have the right to conquer and exploit. Immediately after God gave people dominion over animals (Gen 1:26), he prohibited their use for food (Gen. 1:29). Dominion means guardianship or stewardship—being co-workers with God in taking care of and improving the world.[9]

The Talmud interprets "dominion" as the privilege of using animals for labor only,[10] and this privilege was carefully guarded by laws to protect the animals. The concept of dominion does not permit breeding animals and treating them as machines designed solely to meet our needs.

Rabbi Kook states that dominion does not in any way imply the rule of a haughty despot who tyrannically governs for his own personal selfish ends and with a stubborn heart.[11] He states that he cannot believe that such a repulsive form of servitude could be forever sealed in the world of God whose "tender mercies are over all His work."[12]

Rabbi Hirsch stresses that people have not been given the right or the power to have all creatures subservient to them. In commenting on Genesis 1:26, he states, "The earth and its creatures may have other relationships of which we are ignorant, in which they serve their own purpose."[13] Thus, above people's control over nature there is a divine program to serve God's purposes and objectives, and people have no right to interfere. Hence, people, according to Judaism, do not have an unlimited right to use and abuse animals and other parts of nature.

Question 5. If God wanted us to have vegetarian diets and not harm animals, why were the Temple sacrificial services established?

Answer. During the time of Moses, it was the general practice among all nations to worship by means of sacrifice.[14] There were many associated idolatrous practices. The great Jewish philosopher Maimonides states that God did not command the Israelites to give up and discontinue all these manners of service because "to obey such a commandment would have been contrary to the nature of man, who generally cleaves to that to which he is used,"[15] For this reason, God allowed Jews to make sacrifices, but "He transferred to His service that which had served as a worship of created beings and of things imaginary and unreal."[16] All elements of idolatry were removed. Maimonides concludes:

> By this divine plan it was effected that the traces of idolatry were blotted out, and the truly great principle of our Faith, the Existence and Unity of God, was firmly established; this result was thus obtained without deterring or confusing the minds of the people by the abolition of the service to which they were accustomed and which alone was familiar to them.[17]

The Jewish philosopher Abarbanel reinforces Maimonides's argument. He cites a *Midrash* that indicated that the Jews had become accustomed to sacrifices in Egypt. To wean them from these idolatrous practices, God tolerated the sacrifices but commanded that they be offered in one central sanctuary:[18]

> Thereupon the Holy One, blessed be He, said "Let them at all times offer their sacrifices before Me in the Tabernacle, and they will be weaned from idolatry, and thus be saved."[19]

Rabbi J. H. Hertz, the late chief rabbi of England, states that had Moses not instituted sacrifices, which were admitted by all to have been the universal expression of religious homage, his mission would have failed, and Judaism would have disappeared.[20] With the destruction of the Temple, the rabbis state that prayer and good deeds took the place of sacrifice.

Rashi indicates that God did not command the Israelites to bring certain sacrifices; it was their choice.[21] He bases this on the *haftorah* read on the Sabbath when the first portion of Leviticus, which discusses sacrifices, is read:

> I have not burdened thee with a meal-offering, Nor wearied thee with frankincense. (Isaiah 43:23)

Biblical commentator David Kimchi (1160-1235) also suggests that the sacrifices were never mandatory, but voluntary.[22] He ascertains this from the words of Jeremiah

> For I spoke not unto your fathers, nor commanded them in the day that I brought them out of the land of Egypt, concerning burnt-offerings or sacrifices; but this thing I commanded them, saying, "Obey my voice, and I will be your God, and ye shall be my people; and walk ye in all the ways that I have commanded you, that it may be well unto you. (Jeremiah 7:22-23)

Kimchi notes that nowhere in the Ten Commandments is there any reference to sacrifice, and even when sacrifices are first mentioned (Lev. 1:2) the expression used is "when any man of you bringeth an offering," the first Hebrew word *ki* being literally "if", implying that it was a voluntary act.[23]

Many Jewish scholars such as Rabbi Kook believe that animal sacrifices will not be reinstated in messianic times, even with the reestablishment of the Temple.[24] They believe that at that time human conduct will have advanced to such high standards that there will no longer be need for animal sacrifices to atone for sins. Only nonanimal sacrifices (grains, for example) to express gratitude to God would remain. There is a *Midrash* (teaching based on Jewish values and tradition) that states: "In the Messianic era, all offerings will cease, except the thanksgiving offering, which will continue forever."[25] The abolition of all other sacrifices, along with Rabbi Kook's statement that sacrifices in the future Temple will be vegetarian, are consistent with the belief of Rabbi Kook and others, based on the prophecy of Isaiah (11:6-9), that people and animals will be vegetarian in that time, and "none shall hurt nor destroy in all My Holy mountain."

Sacrifices, especially animal sacrifices, were not the primary concern of God. As a matter of fact, they could be an abomination to Him if not carried out together with deeds of loving kindness and justice. Consider these words of the prophets, the spokesmen of God:

> What I want is mercy, not sacrifice. (Hos. 6:6)
>
> "To what purpose is the multitude of your sacrifices unto Me?" sayeth the Lord. "I am full of the burnt offerings of rams, and the fat of fed beasts; and I delight not in the blood of bullocks, or of lambs or of he-goats...bring no more vain oblations.... Your new moon and your appointed feasts my soul hateth;... and when ye spread forth your hands, I will hide mine eyes from you; yea, when ye make many prayers, I will not hear; your hands are full of blood." (Isa. 1:11-16)
>
> I hate, I despise your feasts, and I will take no delight in your solemn assemblies. Yea, though you offer me burnt-offerings and your meal offerings, I will not accept them neither will I regard the peace-offerings of your fat beasts. Take thou away from me the noise of thy song; and let Me not hear the melody of thy psalteries. But let justice well up as waters, and righteousness as a mighty stream. (Amos 5:21-4)

Deeds of compassion and kindness toward all creation are of greater significance to God than sacrifices: "To do charity and justice is more acceptable to the Lord than sacrifice" (Prov. 21:3).

Perhaps a different type of sacrifice is required of us today:

> When Rabbi Shesheth kept a fast for Yom Kippur, he used to conclude with these words: "Sovereign of the Universe, Thou knowest full well that in the time of the Temple when a man sinned he used to bring a sacrifice, and though all that was offered of it was fat and blood, atonement was made for him. Now I have kept a fast and my fat and blood have diminished. May it be Thy will to account my fat and blood which have been diminished as if I have offered them before thee on the altar, and do Thou favor me."[26]

Question 6. Don't the laws of *shechita* provide for a humane slaughter of animals so that we need not be concerned with violations of *tsa'ar ba'alei chayim*?

Answer. It is true that *shechita* has been found in scientific tests conducted in the United States and other countries to be a relatively painless method of slaughter.[27] But can we consider only the final minutes of an animal's life? What about the tremendous pain and cruelty involved in the entire process of raising and transporting animals? Since, as was shown in chapter 3, the consumption of meat is not necessary and is even harmful to people's health, can any method of slaughter be considered humane? Is this not a contradiction in terms?

No book on Judaism and vegetarianism can be considered complete without a discussion of the very controversial subject of shackling and hoisting.

According to Jewish law an animal must be conscious when brought to the *shochet* for slaughter. Prior to the introduction of shackling and hoisting, the general method of restraining animals before slaughter was to cast them to the floor where they were held in place. In 1906, the U. S. Department of Agriculture ruled that this process was unsanitary because a diseased animal could infect all other animals that came into contact with its blood. Thus the Department ordered that all animals must be lifted off the packing-house floor prior to slaughter.[28] Hence the process of shackling and hoisting, which is *not* a necessary part of the ritual of *shechitah*, was initiated to meet U. S. government requirements, as a means of restraining an animal and positioning it for ritual slaughter.

The problem with shackling and hoisting is that it causes great pain to animals and thus violates the Jewish mandate of *tsa'ar ba'alei chayim*. The process involves placing an iron chain around the hind leg of the animal and hoisting the animal into the air by its hind leg while the rest of the body and head are suspended downward. Even in the comparatively short period in which the animal hangs from its leg it experiences great pain.[29] As indicated before, the *Code of Jewish Law* forbids tying the legs of an animal in a manner that would cause them pain.

Fortunately, there is an alternative, more humane method that is acceptable to Jewish law. Holding pens have been developed to meet the requirements of ritual slaughter and the Department of Agriculture law, while avoiding the use of shackling and hoisting. These pens have been endorsed by the Jewish Joint Advisory Committee on *Shechita*, the Rabbinical Council of America, and several prominent orthodox rabbis.[30]

Because of the high initial costs of holding pens, many slaughterhouses have not adopted them. However, the use of the pens would save slaughterhouses money after a few years because shackling and hoisting sometimes damages the animals and makes the meat unkosher.

Many humane groups have pushed for legislation banning shackling and hoisting. Unfortunately, some anti-Semitic groups have used the issue to discredit *shechita* as well as Jewish law in general. The Jewish community must work for humane alternatives to shackling and hoisting, primarily to be consistent with the mandate to avoid *tsa'ar ba'alei chayim* but also to reduce criticism. Of course, as indicated earlier, the best way to be consistent with Jewish teachings concerning animals is to be a vegetarian.

Question 7. Aren't vegetarians deviating from Jewish tradition in asserting that people and animals are of equal value?

Answer. While some vegetarians believe that people and animals are equal, the vast majority of vegetarians do not.

Concern for animals and a refusal to brutally treat and slaughter them for food that is not necessary and, as a matter of fact, is harmful to human health, does not mean that animals are regarded as equal to people. Also, many people are vegetarians for reasons other than animal rights, such as preservation of health, reduction of ecological threats, and help for hungry people. The vast majority of vegetarians consume milk and eggs and use other animal products such as leather.

It is because humans *are* a superior species that we should behave decently to animals. As author Brigid Brophy (1929-) put it: "We are the species uniquely capable of imagination, rationality, and moral choice - and that is precisely why we are under the obligation to recognize and respect the rights of animals."[30a]

The test of our behavior toward animals should be, as the British philosopher Jeremy Bentham (1748-1832) put it, "not can they reason, nor can they talk, but *can they suffer*?"[30b] And, as indicated in chapter one, Maimonides felt that animals are like people in feeling pain and fleeing from death.

Question 8. Won't a movement by Jews toward vegetarianism mean less emphasis on *kashrut* (the Jewish kosher laws) and eventually a disregard of these laws?

Answer. Not necessarily. One of the purposes of the laws of *kashrut* is to keep alive a reverence for life. This is certainly consistent with vegetarianism. Another purpose is to avoid pagan practices, which often involve much cruelty to animals and people. This too is consistent with vegetarian ideals.

In many ways becoming a vegetarian makes it easier and cheaper to observe the laws of *kashrut*; this might attract many new adherents to keeping kosher and eventually to other important Jewish values. As a vegetarian, one need not be concerned with separate dishes, mixing *milchigs* (dairy products) with *fleishigs* (meat products), waiting 3 or 6 hours after eating meat before being allowed to eat dairy products, storing four sets (two for regular use and two for Passover use) of dishes, silverware, pots, and pans, and many other considerations that must concern the nonvegetarian who wishes to observe *kashrut* strictly. In addition, a vegetarian is in no danger of eating blood or fat, which are prohibited, or the flesh of a nonkosher animal. It should be noted that being a vegetarian does not automatically guarantee that one will maintain the laws of *kashrut* as, for example, certain baked goods and cheeses may not be kosher. When in doubt, of course, a trusted rabbinic authority should be consulted.

A growing problem on the American Jewish scene today is the increasing questioning of kashrut supervision.[31] There have been rumors that even reliable kashrut supervisors have made mistakes.[32] A recent issue of the *Jewish Press* listed 84 food establishments that paid fines related to violations of the Kosher laws. Some observant Jews have chosen to avoid all possible kashrut problems by not eating meat.

Many people today reject *kashrut* because of the high costs involved. Since a person can obtain proper nourishment at far lower costs with a kosher vegetarian diet, this may prevent the loss of many *kashrut* observers.

In a personal letter to the author, Rabbi Robert Gordis, Professor of Bible at the Jewish Theological Seminary, indicates that he sees little hope that *kashrut* will be maintained by most Jewish people in our day in its present form. He indicates that vegetarianism, the logical consequence of Jewish teaching, would be a way of protecting *kashrut*. He states, "Vegetarianism offers an ideal mode for preserving the religious and ethical values which *kashrut* was designed to concretize in human life."

There are several examples in Jewish history when a change to vegetarianism enabled Jews to adhere to *kashrut*. As indicated earlier, Daniel and his companions were able to avoid eating nonkosher food by adopting a vegetarian diet. The historian Josephus relates how some Jewish priests on trial in Rome ate only figs and nuts to avoid eating flesh that had been used in idol worship.[33] Some Maccabees, during the struggles against the Syrians, escaped to the mountains where they lived on only plant foods to avoid "being polluted like the rest."[34]

Question 9. Isn't a movement toward vegetarianism a movement away from Jewish traditions with regard to diet? Isn't there a danger that once some traditions are changed, others may readily follow, and little will be left of Judaism as we have known it?

Answer. Jewish law is based on a two-part structure: written law (the Torah) and oral law (Talmud, *responsa* literature, and other rabbinic writings). Although the written law remains the unchanging base, the oral law is constantly adapting current conditions into its framework. This system has kept Judaism as alive and applicable today as it was centuries ago. In contemporary times, the vast *responsa* literature of this century has enabled new traditions to form within *halachic* bounds.

A move toward vegetarianism is actually a return to Jewish traditions, to taking Jewish values seriously. A movement toward vegetarianism can help revitalize Judaism. It can show that Jewish values can be applied to help solve current world problems related to hunger, waste, and pollution. This could help attract idealistic Jews. Hence, rather than a movement away from Jewish traditions, it would have the opposite effect.

Question 10. Weren't the Jewish sages aware of the evils related to eating meat? If so, why does so much of talmudic literature discuss laws and customs related to the consumption of meat? Are you suggesting that Judaism has been morally wrong in not advocating vegetarianism?

Answer. Conditions today differ greatly from those in biblical times and throughout most of Jewish history. Only recently has strong medical evidence linked a meat-centered diet to many types of disease. Modern farming methods lead to conditions quite different from those that prevailed previously. To produce meat today, animals are treated very cruelly, they are fed tremendous amounts of grains while millions of people starve, and there are many problems related to pollution and resource scarcities. When it was felt that eating meat was necessary for health and the many negative conditions related to intensive raising of animals did not exist, the Jewish sages were not morally wrong in not advocating vegetarianism.

Question 11. Isn't there a danger that Jews will make a religion of vegetarianism, in effect becoming more vegetarian than Jewish?

Answer. Fortunately we don't have an "either/or" situation here, either Judaism or vegetarianism. Jewish vegetarians are not placing so-called vegetarian values above Torah principles. They are saying that it is basic Jewish values and mandates (to act with compassion to animals, guard our health, share with the hungry, protect the environment, conserve resources, and seek peace) which point strongly to vegetarianism, especially in view of the harm done by modern methods of raising animals on factory farms. They are certainly not saying that Torah values should be rejected but why don't we put these splendid values into practice. Far from rejecting Judaism, they are challenging Jews to live up to Judaism's glorious teachings.

Question 12. Aren't vegetarians being more righteous than God, since God gave permission to eat meat?

Answer. No. As previously documented, there is no obligation to eat meat today. Also, God's first dietary law (Gen. 1:29) was strictly vegetarian and according to Rav Kook and others, the Messianic Epoch will be vegetarian.

Jewish vegetarians believe their diet is most consistent with God's desires that we protect our health, be kind to animals, share with hungry people, protect the environment, and conserve resources. Rather than being more righteous than God, they are urging people to live up to God's highest ideals.

This viewpoint is conceded by Rabbi Alfred Cohen:

> If a person tends toward vegetarianism because he sees it as a lifestyle consonant with the way the All-Mighty really wanted the world to be, there can be no denying that he has a valid point of view.[35]

Question 13. How can you advocate making changes in Judaism?
Answer. Rabbinic enactments to meet changing conditions have historically been part of Judaism. In the past Jews practiced polygamy, for example. As Israel Zangwill put it, "Like a language, a religion was dead when it ceased to change."[36] Of course changes must be consistent with Jewish values and teachings.

What is really advocated is not a change but a return, a return to Jewish values of showing compassion, sharing, helping the needy, preserving the environment, conserving resources, and seeking peace.

Finally, global threats today - pollution, hunger, resource scarcity, violence - are so great that a new thinking or rethinking about values and new methods is necessary. As Albert Einstein expressed it, "The unleashed power of the atom has changed everything except our ways of thinking; hence we drift toward unparalleled catastrophe."[37]

Jewish vegetarians are not advocating changes in the Torah, but that the Torah be applied to master preent world conditions, as it has in the past. Global survival today requires a return to Torah values.

Question 14. Wasn't Genesis 1:29 (the first dietary law) overridden by later Torah commandments and teachings?

Answer. As indicated previously, while God's original intention was that people be vegetarians, God later gave permission for meat to be eaten as a reluctant concession to people's weakness. As also indicated, many Biblical commentators look at vegetarianism as the ideal diet, and modern science has verified that our body structure and digestive system are most consistent with this type of diet.

In the *responsum* previously referred to, R. Moshe Halevi Steinberg expressed his belief that the fact that meat was initially forbidden and later permitted indicates that each person is thereby given a free hand to either be a vegetarian as was the first human, or to eat all kinds of food, as Noah did.

The question is then on what basis should that choice be made. Should it be on the basis of convenience, habit, and conformity, or based on consideration of basic Jewish values and teachings?

Rabbi Alfred Cohen indicates, "the Torah does not establish the eating of meat as a desirable activity, only as something which is not forbidden to do."[38] As a matter of fact, the less meat eaten the better; one who eats meat too often is called a "glutton", though he or she is within the technical limits of the Torah.

Rabbi Israel Salanter (1810-1883) felt that talmudic laws relating to the consumption of meat on the Sabbath were for the benefit of the poor, who depended on charity to appease their hunger. Hence the needy would be provided what was then considered nutritious food, at least once a week.[39]

Question 15. While vegetarians are not violating *halacha* by not eating meat, isn't their failure to eat meat at least on *Yom Tov* (holidays) and the Sabbath in violation of the spirit of Jewish law?

Answer. This question is based on the fact that many Jewish sages felt that one could experience joy only by eating meat on holidays. Maimonides, for example, states that "...there is no joy except with meat and wine."[40]

Once again we must recognize the tremendous changes that have occurred in livestock agriculture and our medical knowledge. Maimonides was not aware of health problems related to the consumption of meat, and these problems have become far worse. In the time of our sages, animals were not raised under horrible conditions on factory farms, and modern problems related to the production of meat such as widespread hunger, ecological threats, and resource scarcities were not prevalent.

Since we are, or should be, aware of these modern problems, it is vegetarian diets that are most consistent with the *spirit* of Jewish tradition and values.

It should be noted that, while in the days of the talmudic sages vegetarians were generally ascetics who rejected life's joys, today vegetarianism is viewed as life-sustaining and life-enhancing.

It is also important to note (1) that the above quote from Maimonides fails to include the Talmudic qualifier in *Pesachim* 109a that the obligation to eat meat to rejoice on holidays only held "in the time when the Temple is standing", and (2) that earlier in the same quote, Maimonides indicates that people rejoice in different ways: sweets and nuts for children and new clothing for women.

Question 16. Because the majority of Jews will probably continue to eat meat, isn't it better that they do so without being aware of the Jewish principles such as *bal tashchit, tsa'ar ba'alei chayim*, and *pikuach nefesh* that are being violated? Shouldn't a Jewish vegetarian abstain from meat quietly and not try to convert others to his type of diet?

Answer. This is a common attitude that the author has found. Many people feel that if there are benefits to vegetarianism and if some people want to have such a diet, fine. But they should keep it to themselves and not try to convert others.

The question really becomes one of how seriously we take Jewish values. Are we to ignore Torah mandates to preserve our health, show compassion for animals, not waste, help feed the hungry, preserve the earth, and many others that are violated directly or indirectly by meat-centered diets? Is it proper that people be kept uninformed about the many violations of Torah law so that they can continue their eating habits with a clear conscience?

Judaism teaches that one should try to teach others and assist them to carry out commandments. The importance of speaking out when improper actions are occurring[41] is indicated by the following powerful talmudic teaching:

> Whoever is able to protest against the transgressions of his own family and does not do so is punished for the transgressions of his family. Whoever is able to protest against the transgressions of the people of his community and does not do so is punished for the transgressions of his community. Whoever is able to protest against the transgressions of the entire world and does not do so is punished for the transgressions of the entire world.[42]

The Talmud also relates a story of how apparently righteous individuals were punished along with the wicked because "they had the power to protest but they did not."[43]

Related to these principles are the following teachings of the Jewish sages:

> If a man of learning participates in public affairs and serves as judge or arbiter, he gives stability to the land. But if he sits in his home and says to himself, "What have the affairs of society to do with me?... Why should I trouble myself with the people's voices of protest? Let my soul dwell in peace!" If he does this, he overthrows the world.[44]

> If the community is in trouble, a man must not say, "I will go to my house, and eat and drink, and peace shall be with thee, O my soul." But a man must share in the trouble of his community, even as Moses did. He who shares in its troubles is worthy to see its consolation.[45]

Question 17. How would a Jewish vegetarian celebrate Passover?

Answer. Today there is no need to eat or cook meat on Passover. The eating of the Paschal lamb is no longer required now that the Temple has been destroyed. One is required to commemorate this act, not to participate in it. The late Dayan Feldman stated that mushrooms, which have a fleshy appearance, can be used on the seder plate to commemorate the Pascal lamb.[46] The Talmud indicates that a broiled beet can be used.[47]

The proper celebration of Passover requires the absence of leaven and the use of unleavened bread, which we are commanded to eat "throughout your generations." There are many vegetarian recipes that are appropriate for seders and other Passover meals, a number of which can be found in chapter 8 and several books in the bibliography, especially No Choles-*terol Passover Recipes* by Debra Wasserman and Charles Stahler.

Because Passover is the celebration of our redemption from slavery, we should also consider freeing ourselves from the slavery to harmful eating habits. As our homes are freed from leaven, perhaps we should also free our bodies from harmful foods. Because Passover is a time of regeneration, physical as well as spiritual, the maximum use should be made of raw fruits and vegetables, which have cleansing properties.

There are other Passover themes related to vegetarian ideas. The call at the seders for "all who are hungry to come and eat" is a reminder that our diets can be a factor in reducing global starvation. The Passover theme of freedom is relevant to the horrible conditions of slavery under which animals are raised today.

The recently published *Haggadah for the Liberated Lamb* (see bibliography) provides many excellent ideas and concepts related to the holiday motif of freedom that can supplement the traditional Haggadah.

Question 18. In Jewish literature, it is stated that with the advent of the Messiah a banquet will be given by God to the righteous at which the flesh of the giant fish, Leviathan, will be served.[48] Isn't this inconsistent with the idea that the messianic period will be vegetarian?

Answer. These legends concerning the Leviathan are interpreted as allegories by most commentators.[49] According to Maimonides, the banquet is an allusion to the spiritual enjoyment of the intellect.[50] Abarbanel and others consider the expressions about the Leviathan to be allusions to the destruction of the powers that are hostile to the Jews.[51]

Question 19. Isn't much of Judaism today related to the use of animals for teaching and ritual purposes? (Consider the Sefer Torah, Tefillin, the shofar (ram's horn used on Rosh Hashanah and at the end of Yom Kippur), etc.).

Answer. The number of animals slaughtered for these purposes is minute compared to the billions killed annually for food. The fact that there would still be some animal slaughter to meet Jewish ritual needs shouldn't stop us from doing all we can to end the horrible abuses of factory farming. Also, most problems related to flesh-centered diets - poor human health, waste of food and other resources, and ecological threats - would not occur if animals were slaughtered only to meet Jewish ritual needs. In addition, for *hiddur* (enhancement of) *mitzvah*, it would be better if ritual objects were made from animals who at least led happy, healthy lives, rather than from animals who suffered so terribly.

Question 20. Some people believe that vegetarians are supposed to aspire to become vegans (people who don't use milk, eggs, leather, honey, or any product from an animal). How can an orthodox Jew be a vegan since he would not be able to use tefillin, or shofar, a sefer Torah and other ritual items?

Answer. If a person became a vegetarian but not a vegan, he or she would still do much good for animals, the environment, hungry people, and the preservation of his or her health.

If a person became a vegan except in cases where specific *mitzvot* require use of some animal product, even more good would be done.

Our emphasis should be on doing a minimum amount of harm to other people, the environment, and other animals. The fact that some animal products are required for sacred uses (a very small amount) should not prevent a person from becoming a vegetarian.

Question 21. What about the Kabbalistic concept, prevalent among Chassidim that, if one is religious and performs Torah mitzvot, that person elevates the soul of the animal by consuming its flesh since the energy produced from the animal is used to perform mitzvot which the animal could not perform in any other way?

Answer. This concept is related to the following important kabbalistic teachings: during the Creation process, the Holy Vessels (*sephirot*) which were intended to contain the Holy Light were shattered. Sparks of holiness fell into lower levels of consciousness, becoming entrapped in material things. Mitzvot are a way of "elevating" these sparks back into their proper place in the universe. When done with the proper *kavannah* (intention), *mitzvot* elevate "psychic energy" from the material world back to the Creator. This process called *tikkun olam*, ("repairing the universe") will lead to the coming of Moshiach. Chassidim see meat eating as part of this process since they believe the animals are thus elevated into holiness.

Rabbi Yonassan Gershom, a modern vegetarian chassidic rebbe, believes that this concept can be reconciled with vegetarianism. He feels that the process of raising sparks is cumulative rather than self-perpetuating, and that the recent increase in vegetarianism and the complete absence of holiness in the kosher meat industry today mean that the process of raising sparks through eating animals has been completed. After visiting a slaughterhouse, he asserts that *shochtim*, as sincere as they may be, can't maintain a holy consciousness while slaughtering hundreds of animals or thousands of birds day in and day out. Hence, he asserts, we are now left with the empty shell of fleshpots without holiness. Reb Gershom concludes that, "in this century, to become a vegetarian is to help bring Moshiach."

As a non-chassid, I would add, respectfully, that it seems hard to see how animals can be elevated today through a process that involves so much cruelty and does so much harm to individuals and the world. Also, in view of current nutrition studies, wouldn't one be better able to perform mitzvot and other activities through a sensible, nutritious vegetarian diet, rather than by eating meat, with all its harmful additives?

Question 22. When the Temple in Jerusalem is rebuilt, won't the sacrificial services be restored, and won't people have to eat meat?

Answer. As indicated previously, Rav Kook and others believe that in the Messianic epoch, human conduct will have improved to such a degree that animal sacrifices will not be necessary to atone for sins. There will only be non-animal sacrifices to express thanks to God.

As also indicated, based on the prophecy of Isaiah (11:6-9) Rav Kook and others believe that the Messianic period will be vegetarian.

While most Jewish scholars assume that all Jews ate meat during the time that the Temple stood, it is significant that some (*Tosafot, Yoma* 3a, and Rabbenu Nissim, *Sukkah* 42b)[52] assert that even during the Temple period it was not an absolute requirement to eat meat! Rabbenu Nissim characterizes the "requirement" to eat the meat of festival offerings as *mitzvah min ha-muvchar*, that is, the optimal way of fulfilling the mitzvah of rejoicing on the festival, but *not* an absolute requirement.[53]

R. Moshe Halevi Steinberg, in the *responsum* previously mentioned, points out that vegetarianism for health reasons did not conflict with *halacha* even in Temple times.[54] He indicates that one could be a vegetarian the whole year, and by eating a *kazayit* (olive-size portion which, due to its size, would not damage his health) of meat, he would fulfill the *mitzva* of eating the meat of sacrifices. Even a *kohen* (priest) could be vegetarian except when his turn came to eat of the sacrifices during his period of duty (about 2 weeks), when he, too, could eat just a *kazayit*. He actually could eat even less according to the Hatam Sofer, since many *kohanim* could join together to eat the required amount, so that the vegetarian *kohen* could eat even less than a *kazayit*.[55] R. Steinberg notes that, among the things listed as disqualifying a *kohen* from service in the Temple, vegetarianism is not included, since he could arrange the problem of the eating of the sacrifices in one of the ways listed above. However, R. Steinberg adds, a *kohen* who became a vegetarian because his soul recoiled against eating meat would not have been allowed to serve in the sanctuary since, if he forced himself to swallow a *kaza*yit of meat, it would not fulfill the halachic definition of "eating".

Question 23. What would happen to butchers, *shochtim*, and others dependent for a livelihood on the consumption of meat?

Answer. There could be a shift from the production of flesh products to that of nutritious vegetarian dishes. In England during World War II, when there was a shortage of meat, butchers relied mainly on the sale of fruits and vegetables. Today, new businesses could sell such food products as tofu, miso, felafel, soyburgers, and vegetarian cholent.

The change to vegetarianism would probably be gradual. This would provide time for a transition to other jobs. Some of the funds saved by individuals and groups because of lower food and health costs should be used to provide incomes for people during the retraining period.

The same kind of question can be asked about other moral issues. What would happen to all the arms merchants if we had universal peace? What would happen to doctors and nurses if people took better care of themselves, stopped smoking, improved their diets, and so on? Immoral or inefficient practices should not be supported by pointing out that some people earn a living from them.

Question 24. What if everyone became vegetarian? Wouldn't animals overrun the earth?

Answer. This concern is based on an insufficient understanding of animal behavior, both natural and under present factory conditions. There are not millions of turkeys around at Thanksgiving because they want to help celebrate the holiday but because farmers want them to exist. The breeders, not the animals themselves, control the breeding behavior and thus the number of stock. Recent studies have shown that animals, in natural conditions, adjust their numbers to fit their environment and food supply. An end to the distortion of the sex lives of animals to suit our needs would lead to a decrease, rather than an increase, in animals.[56]

We are not overrun by the animals that we do not eat, such as lions, elephants, and crocodiles. The problem often is that of the extinction of animals, rather than their overrunning the earth. There are many meat-bearing animals today because they are raised under rigid breeding-controlled environments.

Question 25. Instead of advocating vegetarianism, shouldn't we try to alleviate the evils of the factory farming system so that animals are treated better, less grain is wasted, and fewer health-harming chemicals are used?

Answer. The breeding of animals is a big business, whose prime concern is profit. Animals are raised the way they are today because it increases profits. Improving conditions as suggested by this question would certainly be a step in the right direction, but it would be strongly resisted by the meat industry and, if successful, would greatly increase already high prices.

Here are two counter questions. Why not abstain from eating meat as a protest against present policies while trying to improve them? Even under the best of conditions, why take the life of a creature of God, "whose tender mercies are over all His creatures," when it is not necessary for proper nutrition?

At the request of people in Minnesota who wanted meat but were concerned about cruelty to animals and chemicals in their food, Rabbi Yonassan Gershom investigated the possibility of locating organically raised kosher animals and free-running kosher chickens. He found that they are almost non-existent. He concludes that the only humane and healthy alternative is to be a kosher vegetarian.

Question 26. Isn't it important that we keep our priorities straight? How can we be so concerned about animals when there are so many critical problems related to people today?

Answer. Certainly many critical issues face the world today; that is why I have written two other books, *Judaism and Global Survival*, and *Mathematics and Global Survival*, which address current world problems.

There is an ecological principle that "everything is connected to everything else." This means that every action has many ramifications. Hence, adopting vegetarian diets not only reduces brutal treatment of animals; it also improves human health, reduces stress on threatened ecosystems, conserves resources, and provides the potential to reduce widespread hunger. In view of the many threats related to livestock agriculture, next to attempting to reduce the chance of nuclear war, working to promote vegetarianism may be the most important action one can take for global survival.

While it is true that there are people who love animals but are cruel to people, some of history's greatest humanitarians were vegetarians. These include: Plutarch, Leonardo da Vinci, Sir Isaac Newton, Jean Jacques Rousseau, General William Booth, Ralph Waldo Emerson, Henry David Thoreau, Percy Bythe Shelley, Dr. J. H. Kellogg, Horace Greeley, Susan B. Anthony, Leo Tolstoy, Upton Sinclair, H. G. Wells, George Bernard Shaw, Albert Schweitzer, and Mahatma Gandhi.[57]

Question 27. How does vegetarianism relate to vivisection (experiments on animals)? Don't we need this for improved human health?

Answer. As indicated previously, the Torah mandates that we show compassion to animals. However, in Judaism, as in most of the world's leading religions, animals are not considered equal to human beings. The

Jewish tradition sanctions animal experiments that benefit humans, as long as unnecessary pain is avoided. The question thus becomes one of whether or not people are really benefited and if other methods are available.

Since many laboratory experiments on animals are designed to discover cures for diseases related to our high consumption of flesh foods, wouldn't a switch to vegetarian diets do more for human health? Are we justified in having a diet which requires horribly cruel treatment of animals, and then to brutally mistreat millions of other animals to seek cures for illnesses related to that diet? Isn't it better not to have a heart attack than to have an artificial heart?

Many laboratory experiments are completely unnecessary. Must we force dogs to smoke to reconfirm the health hazards of cigarettes? Do we have to starve dogs and monkeys to understand human starvation? Do we need to cut, blind, burn, and chemically destroy animals to produce still another type of lipstick, mascara, or shampoo?

Do experiments performed on animals always produce results which are valid for people? There is an ever-growing list of drugs that were deemed safe after very extensive animal testing which later proved to be carcinogenic, mutagenic (causing birth defects) or toxic (poisonous) to humans. Conversely, penicillin, our most useful antibiotic, is toxic to many animal species, and common aspirin is deadly to cats.

A reduction of animal experiments does not mean that experiments have to be done on people. Healthier lifestyles would avoid the need for many experiments. Also, many new approaches to advancing scientific knowledge have been developed. Dr. Fred Rosner, a modern expert on Jewish medical ethics, states that if alternate means, e.g. tissue culture studies, are available for obtaining the same information, animal experimentation might be considered as unnecessary cruelty to animals and be prohibited.[58] Dr. Rosner also indicates that animal experiments would not be permitted simply to satisfy intellectual curiosity.[59]

Question 28. Can't one work to improve conditions for animals without being a vegetarian?

Answer. Certainly. But it must be noted that the number of warm blooded animals brutalized and slaughtered for food annually is about 30 times the number of animals killed by hunters and trappers, 70 times the number killed in laboratories, and 500 times the number killed in animal pounds.[60] You might be helping some animals but, if you eat meat, an average of 22 warm-blooded animals are killed for your food each year.[61]

Question 29. Isn't it really necessary to eat meat to get sufficient protein and other nutrients?

Answer. Experts in dietetics are best qualified to answer this question. Hence the following conclusions of the American Dietetic Association are significant:

> 1. "...well planned vegetarian diets are consistent with good nutritional status."[62]
>
> 2. "...most of mankind for much of human history has subsisted on near-vegetarian diets."[63]
>
> 3. "...a growing body of scientific evidence supports a positive relationship between the consumption of a plant-based dietary and the prevention of certain diseases."[64]

Most people consume two or three times the protein that they need and this has negative health consequences.

Chapter 8 presents many ideas and recipes for proper nutrition.

Question 30. Are there any steps for improving health beyond vegetarianism?

Answer. A comprehensive approach is natural hygiene, the study of the science of natural living. A complete discussion of this topic is beyond the scope of this book.[65] In addition to vegetarianism, natural hygiene promotes proper exercise, rest, sleep, and emotional poise. It stresses the use of fresh ripe fruits and vegetables, nuts, seeds, and sprouts as opposed to processed foods or vitamin and mineral supplements.

Further information may be obtained from the American Natural Hygiene Society, P.O. Box 30630, Tampa, Florida 33630.

Question 31. Aren't there also problems related to eating vegetables? Don't vegetables have feelings? Aren't vegetables also sprayed with chemicals?

Answer. The concept of concern for plants is actually a strong positive point for vegetarianism. Because animals have to eat about ten times as much vegetable food to return a single unit of food value as meat, a vegetarian diet means less destruction of plants. Also, most vegetarian food can be obtained without killing the plant; this includes ripe fruits and nuts, berries, melons, seeds, legumes, tomatos, squash, cucumbers, and pumpkins.

It is good that people are starting to realize that plants have a certain state of sensitivity. Perhaps this will lead to a greater awareness that animals are not unfeeling beasts. And certainly the consciousness in plants is of a different quality than that in humans and animals.

Unfortunately, it is true that vegetables are sprayed with many chemicals. It is important to wash them well. Also, efforts should be made to reduce unnecessary spraying of pesticides. But here, too, vegetarianism is beneficial because, as indicated previously, the movement of chemicals up the food chain leads to far greater amounts of pollutants in meat and fish.

Question 32. What is the definition of a vegetarian diet? Can a vegetarian eat fish?

Answer. The generally accepted definition of a vegetarian diet is that it includes no flesh foods; that is, no meat, poultry, or fish.[66] There are three types of vegetarian diets: the lacto-ovo-vegetarian diet, which includes dairy products and eggs; the lacto-vegetarian diet, which includes dairy products but not eggs; and the vegan (pronounced "vee-gan") diet, which uses no dairy products or eggs.[67] Vegans frequently do not use honey and avoid using non-food animal products such as leather, wool, and fur. They base their practice on a belief that it is ethically wrong to kill animals or exploit them in any way and/or for health reasons.

Contrary to some people's beliefs, fish cannot be included in a vegetarian diet. Vegetarians avoid fish because they feel it is unnecessary to destroy living creatures for food that is not necessary for proper nutrition; the extensive pollution of many bodies of water and the magnification of pollution effect through food chains makes the consumption of fish dangerous to health. Potential dangers in breast feeding because of chemicals and pesticides in mothers' milk, primarily owing to the consumption of meat and fish, have already been discussed.[68]

Question 33. Aren't people who abstain from eating meat but who consume eggs and milk being hypocritical?

Answer. Many of the arguments made for not eating meat are valid with regard to eggs and milk, although to a lesser degree. Factory farming also brutalizes egg-laying chickens and milk-cows, wastes resources, and pollutes the environment.

The vegan diet (non-use of any animal products) is a more humane diet.

However, it is estimated that 90 percent of vegetarians today are lacto-ovo vegetarians. Many hope to become vegans eventually.

Rather than looking at vegetarians who consume eggs and milk as hypocrites, I prefer to look at them as people who have made an important ethical decision, often in the face of much opposition and criticism, but who have not yet gone as far as they could in terms of a humane, sensible diet.

Question 34. Isn't it hypocritical for a vegetarian to wear leather shoes and use other leather products?

Answer. It depends upon one's reasons for being a vegetarian. If it is based upon health, for example, it would not be inconsistent.

Some vegetarians use leather products because these are byproducts of slaughter, rather than prime causes of it. Many vegetarians have changed to shoes of natural or synthetic non-animal materials. It will become easier to get such products as the demand for them increases. Some vegetarians are continuing to use leather products only until they wear out; then they will shift to non-leather products. In India, leather products are obtained from animals that died natural deaths.

Question 35. Isn't it better to advocate that people reduce their meat consumption rather than that they become vegetarian? Doesn't Judaism advocate moderation, the golden mean, in such matters, rather than complete abstinence?

Answer. Certainly a reduction of meat consumption would be a step in the right direction. And if all or the vast majority of people did this, it would sharply reduce many of the problems that we have been discussing.

However, as indicated in chapter 3, Rabbi Samson Raphael Hirsch stresses, "even the smallest unnecessary deprivation of strength is accountable to God. Every smallest weakening is partial murder. Therefore you should avoid everything which might possibly injure your health."[69]

Responding to a similar argument with regard to smoking, Rabbi Moses Auerbach, a teacher at Hebrew Teachers College in Baltimore states:

> Only deliberate self-delusion can persuade one that there are "safe" limits in smoking...there is absolutely no safety in moderation, since even a limited intake of cigarette poison can seriously aggravate an existing condition of heart or lung disease. In other words, a person's health may be affected

> without the victim's even being aware of it and under circumstances which have nothing to do with smoking. Yet, while such a disease may still be controlled in the case of non-smokers, it could very well prove fatal to smokers, including those of the "moderate" variety.[70]

Rabbi Auerbach also argues that, even if there is a given point below which there is no risk, the peril of addiction and gradual increases beyond "safe" levels would remain.[71]

The argument for moderate meat consumption would need to address similar concerns before asserting that such a diet is consistent with Jewish values.

Question 36. Wasn't Hitler a vegetarian?

Answer. First, is it relevant what Hitler ate or did not eat? No rational person would cite Hitler's non-smoking to discredit non-smokers, but his alleged vegetarianism is repeated ad nauseam.

Because he suffered from excessive sweatiness and flatulence, Hitler occasionally went on a vegetarian diet. But his primary diet involved eating meat. While the Nazis obeyed Hitler slavishly, there is no record of any other Nazi leader being a vegetarian.

Hitler was not only carnivorous, he was an enemy of vegetarians and banned all organizations that advocated vegetarianism in Germany and the occupied countries - and this when a rational diet would have solved the German food shortage.[72] Recall that Hitler's rationale for war was to acquire 'Lebensraum' - more land for, among other things, meat production. In his definitive biography of Hitler, *The Life and Death of Adolph Hitler*, Ralph Payne mentions his special fondness for Bavarian sausages (p. 346). Other biographers including Albert Speer point out that he also ate ham, liver, and game.[73]

Question 37. I enjoy eating meat. Why should I give it up?

Answer. If one is solely motivated by what will bring pleasure, then perhaps this question cannot be answered. But Judaism is concerned with far more: doing *mitzvot*, performing good deeds, sanctifying occasions, helping feed the hungry, pursuing justice and peace, and so on. The objective in writing this book is to indicate that people who take such Jewish values seriously should become vegetarians.

Even if one is primarily motivated by considerations of pleasure and convenience, the negative health effects of a meat-centered diet should be taken into account. One cannot enjoy life when one is not in good health.

Vegetarians, especially those who have recently changed their diets, are generally on the defensive. They must deal with many questions, such as the ones in this chapter. Those who eat meat have the support of society, and thus they never consider the consequences of their diet. Hence it is vegetarians who are asked to explain the reasons for their diet, rather than those who support the brutal treatment and unnecessary slaughter of animals that a meat-centered diet requires.

Perhaps there are times when vegetarians should take the offensive in conversations with meat eaters. To that end, responses to questions can be used to teach others basic ideas, which can help show the benefits of vegetarianism and its consistency with Jewish values.

Here are some questions that can help politely and respectfully to turn the tables on nonvegetarians: Do you know about the cruelty related to raising animals for food today? Are you aware of the links between meat eating and heart disease, cancer, and other illnesses? Could you visit a slaughterhouse or kill an animal yourself? Do you know that while millions die annually of starvation, most grain grown in the United States and other affluent countries is fed to animals? Are you aware of the consequences of a meat-centered diet with regard to pollution, use of land, water, and other resources, and the increased potential for violence and war? Do you know that vegetarianism is the diet most consistent with Jewish values?

8

In the Camp of Kivrot-Hata'avah

Contributed by Roberta Kalechofsky

(Roberta Kalechofsky writes fiction and nonfiction. She is also the founder of Micah Publications and the author of Haggadah for the Liberated Lamb (Micah), a vegetarian seder. This article initially appeared in the *Reconstructionist.*)

> The meat was still between their teeth, not yet chewed, when the anger of the Lord blazed forth against the people, and the Lord struck the people with a very severe plague. (Num. 11:33)

> Israel was promised bread to the full, but not flesh. Their cry for bread was reasonable, but not for meat, for one can do without it. (Rashi's comment on Exodus 16:8)

In the history of philosophy and morals, vegetarianism is a sleeper, an elusive underpinning to mystical movements, rarely respectable enough, until recently, to merit serious scholarly study. Jewish vegetarianism has fared similarly, though Genesis makes it clear that the Edenic world was vegetarian. Prophetic messianism, as the late Rabbi Kook interpreted the prophets and himself believed, is inseparable from vegetarianism. The threads of earliest vegetarian thought are obscure and probably irrecoverable, but they are persistently there. One traces allusions to the subject and tensions between different social structures, such as farming and shepherding, and shepherding and hunting, in the stories of Cain and Abel and Jacob and Esau.

Some contemporary anthropological evidence supports the view that early paleolithic people were vegetarian — seed and nut gatherers — and only later became hunters. Ashley Montagu believes that the story of the Flood may reflect the transition from vegetarianism to meat eating, and that a catastrophe not unlike the Ice Age demolished plant life and destroyed the old gatherer civilization.[1] Art historian Kenneth Clarke, in an article on the paleolithic cave drawings in southern France, speculates that paleolithic people may not have defined themselves as another species, differentiated from other animals.[2]

It is also possible that humans learned how to hunt from the animals. If so — and we must bear in mind that all of this is speculation on ancient events — then the human race, proud of its position at the evolutionary apex, took a step backwards when it became a predator. At any rate, Genesis 9:3-6 makes clear that this moral and dietary change did not occur because of progress, but is rather a change for the worse in the human condition.

History's first ideological-philosophical argument may have been the conflict between vegetarianism and carnivorism, depicted in the rivalry between Cain and Abel. Though it is Abel's progeny who win that argument, God punishes Cain with exile rather than with death. Cain is "set aside" for a future destiny.

Such an interpretation may seem strange to Jews who have never been encouraged to consider vegetarianism as implicitly Jewish and biblically mandated. Nevertheless, a vegetarian- messianic interpretation of the Cain and Abel episode gains credibility when it is considered in light of prophetic attitudes. Many passages from the prophets regard the animal world with loving concern and remind us that plant nature is sufficiently bountiful for food:

> Fear not, beasts of the field, for the pastures in the wilderness are clothed with grass. The trees have borne their fruit; fig tree and vine yield their strength.
>
> (Joel 2:22)

Since the prophets' condemnation of the sacrificial system is often interpreted to mean a condemnation of "empty sacrifice," one must be grateful for Isaiah's succinct and unequivocal statement: "He who kills an ox is the same as he who slays a person" (66:3).

Early vegetarianism in the biblical and Greek worlds are randomly expressed in the Pythagoreans, Plutarch, the prophets, and elsewhere. Moreover, the communal practice of vegetarianism existed in Europe until the last millennium, in the communities of Ebionites and Albigensis. It is only in the last millennium that the thread has been completely submerged in Western tradition.

HEALTH CONCERNS

It has re-emerged in the century for two pressing reasons, both of which require the Jewish people to take up the argument about the relationship between the human race and the animal world. The contemporary Western world traces its religious sentiments and religious identity to the Bible — which is the guardian and guarantor of our earliest and best thoughts about human responsibility for both the natural and the animal world. And the Bible expresses the concept of stewardship; God's covenant is with the beasts of the field and animal life as well as with human life.

Modern vegetarianism in the Western world, both Jewish and non-Jewish, arises from both legitimate health concerns and a need to search for a different model of human involvement with the earth. The latter emerges from reconsiderations of the scientific model, in which empirical knowledge and efficiency are revered as preeminent values. Horror at what is happening in the animal world, under the conditions of factory farming that turn animals into "biomachines," is a dominant motive in Jewish vegetarianism. It is no more possible to reconcile factory farming with Jewish values than it is possible to reconcile totalitarianism with democracy.

FACTORY FARMING

Factory farming is the term used to describe a system of raising animals in conditions of intense crowding in barns, cages, stalls, or boxes in order to maximize efficiency. Typically, a chicken in this system spends its life in an area the size of a shoe box, and a veal calf in a box approximately its own size, tethered at the neck so that it cannot move. The life cycle of the animals are chemically and hormonally altered not only for profit and convenience, but because disease spreads rapidly in such conditions of overcrowding. Thus, quantities of drugs that are difficult to imagine are used to control disease and to disinfect the excrement. A recent report compiled by the Committee on Government Operations charges that there are 20,000-30,000 animal drugs in current use, that as many as 90% have not been approved by the FDA, and that as many as 4,000 of these drugs may have "potentially adverse effects on animals or humans."[3]

Many doctors and scientists assert that the overuse of antibiotics for animals (as well as in humans) may soon cause a very real crisis in the treatment of human disease. It is rapidly rendering ineffective the use of penicillin, aureomycin, and the tetracycline drugs. The evidence that eating meat is dangerous to our health is by now as accepted in many medical circles as the case against smoking.

MODERN MEAT

Even if modern meat were not contaminated, however, the eating of meat more frequently than on rare occasions would be unhealthy in the modern world. We are the first civilization to combine a gluttony for meat products (contaminated or not) with a sedentary lifestyle, leading to the high incidence of four modern diseases: cancer of the colon, heart disease, high blood pressure, and stroke.

The health hazards of eating "modern meat," as Orville Schell entitled his book on factory farming,[4] are so manifold that we stand on the threshold of Kivrot-hata'avah the site in the wilderness where the Israelites rose in rebellion because of the lack of meat and were punished with plague (Num. 11). Yet rabbis who speak eloquently of the Jewish responsibility to human health shrink from the idea of whispering to their congregations: "It is dangerous to eat meat. It is unsafe. It is hazardous. And even if you perform *shechitah*, the meat remains contaminated. You are eating the meat of sick animals."

But beyond the concern for human health, there is another motive underlying modern Jewish vegetarianism. There is a loathing of the factory farming system, of the brutal application of scientific efficiency to living creatures. This had led many to rethink the legitimacy of exploitative experimentation, and to seek ways to reclaim the sacredness of all life.

Many Jewish and non-Jewish vegetarians look upon vegetarianism as a pledge of this new posture. Modern Jewish vegetarianism arises from an affirmation that *all* life is sacred and that humans are responsible for that life. We have wandered too far from the caring commandment that "you may not muzzle the ox when it treads out the corn in the field." We have wandered into the camp of *Kivrot-hata'avah*, and we are dying of ensuing diseases. The honor of the tradition of *shehitah* is degraded by the acceptance of the ethical brutishness of factory farming.

SACRED EARTH

Modern Jews who have become ethical vegetarians believe that they are returning to the source of Jewish religious thought. They seek to pick up the thread of original Jewish instinct about the earth — that it is sacred because God created it, and that a Jew cannot divide God the Creator from God's Creation. They do not regard vegetarianism as a break with tradition, but as a reaffirmation of a submerged but legitimate Jewish tradition and a return to a historical trend. Louis Berman states the trend admirably:

> Life-sustaining and life-enhancing rather than ascetic, this new vegetarianism fulfills more completely the Biblical commandments to nurture human life and to treat with compassion all that lives.[5]

The *Encyclopaedia Judaica* notes that "meat is never included among the staple diet of the children of Israel, which is confined to agricultural products, of which the constantly recurring expression in the Bible is 'grain and wine and oil' (Deut. 11:14) or the seven agricultural products enumerated in Deut. 8:8."[6] The concept of the "good and fertile land," a land blessed by God, has no images of the abundance of meat for human consumption. Though rabbis point out that the eating of meat is often associated with a joyous occasion, it is more often associated with gluttony, self indulgence, and disaster, as the event at Kibroth-hattaavah foreshadows. The description of God's anger, loathing, and contempt for this request for meat is undisguised:

> Say to the people: Be ready for tomorrow and you shall eat meat, for you have kept whining before the Lord and saying, "If only we had meat to eat! Indeed, we were better off in Egypt!" The Lord will give you meat and you shall eat. You shall eat not one day, not two, not even five days or ten, or twenty, but a whole month, until it comes out of your nostrils and becomes loathsome to you. (Num. 11:18-20)

The consequences here are plague and death.

Louis Berman suggests that the early rabbinic rejection of vegetarianism — a matter that was debated in the Talmud — was a reaction to the growing numbers of ascetic sects, whose practice of vegetarianism was advocated or coupled with the practice of celibacy.

This historic problem is irrelevant today, and it is now time for Jews to resume their sensitive insights into the daily matter of eating. Centuries of Jewish religious practice have accustomed us not to regard food — certainly not the eating of meat — willfully and thoughtlessly, but to regard all food as a gift from God, to be eaten with blessing and prayer. For such reasons, and because Jews have already inherited a tradition of setting aside dairy from meat, Jews are preeminently suited to become vegetarians.[7]

COOKING AS AN ART

Nevertheless, if one has not been a vegetarian, the change reqires readjustments in shopping and cooking habits. One must acquire new skills as well as new insights. Vegetarianism should not be regarded as a form of punishment or deprivation, but as the rediscovery of cooking and eating as fundamentally civilizing arts.

For many Jews, it also means recovering the joy of Jewish holidays, so many of which celebrate agriculture and the seasons. Sukkot and Tu Bishvat invite concentration upon plant and grain products. So too the time from Passover to Shavuot, when pilgrims came to Jerusalem with offerings from the first wheat harvests. Cooking a meatless cholent on Friday and practicing a vegetarian Shabbat as a spiritual identification with the commandment that the ox and the calf shall also rest on Shabbat, returns the Jew to an understanding of Shabbat as one of harmony between the human and the natural world. Judaism allows for manifold ways for the Jew to explore vegetarianism and its relationship to tradition. The time is auspiciously ripe because the matter is urgent and our tradition is there.

Two worthwhile books on the subject are Louis Berman's *Vegetarianism and the Jewish Tradition* and Richard Schwartz's *Judaism and Vegetarianism.* A haggadah for Jewish vegetarians, *Haggadah for the Liberated Lamb*, is available from Micah Publications.[8] *Jewish Vegetarian Cooking*, by Rose Friedman, is available from the International Jewish Vegetarian Society or Thorsons Publishers (New York or England). A cookbook for Passover is available from the Jewish Vegetarian Society[9] in addition to a newsletter with information and recipes for all the holidays.

The argument for modern vegetarianism is conclusive, for we now know that meat protein is not necessary for human health. It is pointless to persist in an act that is cruel to living creatures, human or animal, when it cannot be justified on grounds of health or defense.

But more pressing for the Jew is the prophetic vision of justice and mercy "for the beasts of the field." Factory farming is a modern barbarism which denies that Jewish justice and Jewish mercy are for animals; Jews have the power to avoid this evil by not eating meat.

We do not have to bear arms, contribute money, or engage in acts of civil disobedience to end this evil. We do not have to be saints or heroes. We merely have to change a bad habit and rediscover our first law of kashrut: "See, I have given you every seed and herb and green thing for eating. These shall be yours for food" (Gen. 1:29).

9
B'Tay-Avon: Have a Hearty Appetite!

> And you shall eat and be satisfied and bless the Lord your God for the good land He has given you. (Deuteronomy 8:10)

(Contributed by Dr. Shoshana Margolin)

People who consider adopting a vegetarian life-style—whether for health reasons or ethics invariably ask:

"What will I eat?" "Where will I get my protein?" "Will I go througlife with a feeling of deprivation and not being full?"

Nothing will answer these questions more positively than delicious, nourishing and well-planned vegetarian meals. This chapter gives guidelines that can ease initiation into this new world of "harmless eating"—harmless to your own health and harmless because there is no bloodshed involved.

Consider the aesthetics: you walk into a butcher shop, you see the bleeding carcasses hanging on hooks and parts of animal bodies being cut, weighed, and chopped. You notice the blood-stained apron and hands of the butcher. You smell the odor of death, of decomposing flesh. All these are very appetizing to a lion, whose constitution is suited for this fare, but most people—yes, even meat eaters—find it repulsive or at least unappealing.

To be made appetizing, meat must be softened by cooking and the smell and taste disguised with spices and vegetables. When we poll meat eaters at random and ask if they would eat meat provided they had to slaughter animals themselves, we discover many vegetarians-at-heart. The act of preying and tearing flesh is appropriate only for animals with claws and fangs, the carnivorous animals. Most people would *not* enjoy a trip to the slaughterhouse; many shudder at the sight of suffering.

Compare the butcher shop or slaughterhouse with the sight of fruits and vegetables displayed for sale—the lively colors of red, green, yellow, orange, and purple, the aroma of oranges, of ripe peaches, of Golden Delicious apples, of ripe bananas! Don't you find it appetizing just the way it is? Wouldn't you eat fruit even if you had to pick your own? The answers to these questions would be very different from answers to equivalent questions at the butcher shop. Most people *enjoy* picking fruit, vegetables, and berries. They *enjoy* spending time on a fruit farm. They may even note the perfect fit between their palms and the shape of the fruit, as if these were designed for each other.

When you think of it—even without considering the strong evidence of comparative anatomy—it makes sense that a species of creatures will find *appetizing* to its senses (sight, smell, touch, and taste) those foods that are suited for it by original design. To illustrate this point, monkeys find bananas naturally appealing, or else they would not eat them. So it is with other animals: they need not go to school to learn their natural diet; their senses tell them! They don't disguise the flavor by cooking, broiling, baking, sauteeing, steaming, marinating, or by using spice or smoke. They love their food naturally just the way it is! We humans, however, have gotten so far from our source (perhaps the expulsion from the Garden of Eden had a deep dietary significance!) that many of us have lost our instincts completely or at least have aberrated them. Our distorted perceptions are clearly depicted by the prophet Isaiah: "Woe unto them who call evil good, and good evil...that change bitter into sweet and sweet into bitter." (Isaiah 5:20)

Let us regain our senses so that we no longer allow cancer-causing junk food to be labeled "kosher" but return this word to its *complete* original meaning—"fit to eat." It is time for us to expand our consciousness by returning to the natural diet for which our bodies were designed and to reap the many rewards.

A. A WAY OF LIFE

Vegetarianism is relevant only when practiced. If it includes orientation to better health, it will probably be practiced longer (as healthy habits have a definite effect on life span).

Some suggestions for making the transition to vegetarianism and a healthier life-style easier follow. (Remember, you know yourself best; adopt suggestions and pace of change most comfortable for you.)

(1) Many people become vegetarians instantly, totally giving up meat, fish, and poultry overnight. Others make the change gradually. Do what works best for you.

(2) It is important to supply your nutritional needs by eating a wide variety of foods in season rather than to depend on a limited selection of foods with which you were previously familiar. Experiment with new foods, dare to improvise! When using God's bounty in natural form, you can't make serious mistakes.

(3) If possible, plan menus in advance. Take time to build attractive meals using foods you enjoy. Besides recipes given later in this chapter, you can find good vegetarian recipes in the *Jewish Vegetarian* and in books listed in the bibliography. Generally aim to have simple meals with quick and easy preparation. Simplicity in diet has many advantages, including health and saving time.

(4) Approach each meal with positive expectations. Enjoy your food. Don't consider yourself an ascetic. Realize that your diet is best for life—your life and that of spared animals, hungry people, and the environment.

(5) Learn principles of sound nutrition. Read books on vegetarianism and natural health. Start to build a home library that you can use to look up questions as well as to lend books to friends. Subscribe to health magazines, such as *Health Science*, *Vegetarian Voice*, *Vegetarian Journal*, *Prevention*, *Vegetarian Times*, *Bestways* and *East West Journal*. Attend vegetarian and natural health meetings and conferences.

(6) Become familiar with vegetarian restaurants in your area. The *Annual Directory of Vegetarian Restaurants* is available from Daystar Publishing Company, P.O. Box 707, Angwin, CA

94508. Find out which restaurants offer salad bars with a wide variety of fresh vegetables. If you observe laws of *kashrut*, check a restaurant's acceptability.

(7) Associate with other vegetarians and become friendly with health-minded people for mutual support and reinforcement. This is valuable even if socialization is mostly by telephone. It is especially important for children—they must know that there are others like them.

(8) Become familiar with local health food stores, co-ops, ethnic stores, and the natural food section of your supermarket. However, many "natural food" products may be overpriced and not even healthy. You don't have to shop in a special store to obtain healthy vegetarian foods. However, new foods can add variety to your diet. Here are some special items that you should get to know.

Tamari—a natural soy sauce prepared without caramel coloring or chemicals. Some brands are high in salt.
Tahini—natural sesame butter. (*Erewhon* is a good brand.)
Tofu—soy bean curd, which is a high-protein product that can be adapted to many vegetarian dishes.
Rice cakes—puffed brown rice pressed to form round cakes, which are crisp and crunchy.
Unsulfured dried fruits.
Unsalted shelled nuts and seeds.

While no special equipment is necessary for vegetarian diets, the following may be very valuable: a vegetable juicer, blender, food processor, and a stainless steel steamer (with perforated "wings" that open to any size pot and three legs, so water does not touch the vegetables).

(9) Increase consumption of fruits, vegetables, and their freshly squeezed juices. See to it that a good variety of these foods, as well as seeds, raisins, and nuts, are always available at home.

(10) As long as sufficient calories are consumed daily, protein needs can be easily met by all healthy vegetarians and "vegans." Protein and vegetarianism was first closely analysed in *Diet for a Small Planet* by Frances Moore Lappe'. Although this book introduced many important vegetarian concepts, the theory of complementing proteins proved to be misleading, and was later revoked by the author in an updated edition.

Maintaining a healthy diet is simple. The important thing is to eat a variety of wholesome foods including some protein-rich foods and consume sufficient calories.

A few good sources of protein: low-fat dairy products, nuts, seeds, lentils, tofu, tempeh, eggs. Many common foods such as whole grain bread, greens, potatoes, corn and peas add to protein intake.

(11) Use healthier substitutes: Instead of polished rice, use brown rice. Instead of white flour, use whole wheat or brown rice meal. Instead of sugar or an artificial sweetener, use rice bran syrup, or blackstrap molasses. Instead of chocolate or cocoa, use carob powder. Instead of margarine, use sesame oil (in recipes) or Tahini dressing as a spread. Instead of commercial oils, use sesame oil or olive oil.

(12) When you are invited to a wedding, bar mitzvah, or dinner at someone's home, let your hosts know beforehand that you eat only vegetarian food. Generally, they comply cordially. If they ask, "why?," use this as an opportunity to educate them, using the concepts in this and other vegetarian books.

(13) Some additional valuable suggestions for healthy eating are:

Become a label reader; pay special attention to small print on food packages. Minimize use of products with food colorings, preservatives, stabilizers and artificial flavors.
Minimize and aim to avoid the use of foods that contain caffeine, such as coffee, cola drinks, chocolate, and regular tea.

Minimize use of salt, sugar, and artifical sweeteners.
Try to avoid use of aluminum cookware and "silver" foil (which is really aluminum foil). The best cookware to use is Pyrex, Corningware, enamel (if not chipped), and stainless steel, in this order.
Minimize frying.

These suggestions are just a beginning. As you read, attend meetings and interact with like-minded individuals, you will expand your horizons and find the life-style ideal for you.

B. RECIPES

Ideally, a vegetarian diet should not contain canned products, refined sugar and flour, or salt. However, when you first adopt a vegetarian diet, you may not wish to give up all of these immediately. Some of the following recipes take this into account.

**Note: Where recipe calls for eggs, use range free eggs or an egg replacement recipe (preferably the latter). Inquire about either of these from your local health foodstore, animal rights or vegetarian society, or from the North American Jewish Vegetarian Society, P.O.B. 1463, Baltimore, MD (1-301-366-VEGE) for latest information about eggs.*

By picking one ingredient from each column in you can create over 260,000 different salad combinations, enough to last over 700 years if you use a different one each day. As you may choose more than one ingredient from each column, there are almost an infinite number of salad combinations.

Ingredients for Mix-Match Salad

Greens (1 1/2 cups)	*Color* (2 tbsp.)	*Flavor* (to taste)	*Protein* (2-4 oz.)	*Texture* (1 tbsp.)	*Dressing* (about 1/4 cup)
Iceberg lettuce	Tomatoes	Cucumber slice	Cheese	Radishes	Mayonnaise
Romaine lettuce	Red cabbage	Raisins	Hard-cooked eggs	Carrot chunks	Creamy french
Boston lettuce	Diced red apples	Onion rings	Sunflower seeds	Croutons	Russian
Raw spinach	Red pepper	Sauerkraut	Tofu	Celery slices	Thousand Island
Chinese cabbage	Stuffed olives	Garlic (rub bowl)	Walnuts	Green peppers	Oil and tamari
Escarole	Black olives	Diced pickles	Cooked beans	Water chestnuts	Yogurt
Cabbage	Grated carrots	Watercress	Toasted almonds	Pretzel sticks	Sour cream
Chicory	Pickled beets	Chutney	Soy nuts	Sprouts	Blue cheese

Loretta's Nutty Casserole

1 cup chopped nuts (peanuts
 or cashews)
1 cup chopped onion
1 cup chopped celery
1 cup chopped mushrooms
1 cup fine egg noodles
1 cup Chinese noodles
2 cups vegetable stock
 (or boullion)
2 tablespoons oil

Place oil in casserole dish. Mix all other ingredients. Bake, covered, for 1 hour at 350 F.

Vegetarian Nut Loaf

1 1/2 cups chopped peanuts, walnuts,
 or cashews
2 grated carrots
2 cups finely sliced celery
1 cup chopped onion
1/4 cup wheat germ
4 ounces mushrooms
1 cup whole wheat bread crumbs
3 eggs or 3/4 cup egg substitute
1 cup chopped eggplant,
 cauliflower, or green beans
1 can condensed tomato or cream
 of mushroom soup, undiluted

Combine all ingredients, mixing thoroughly. Bake in greased loaf pan at 400 F for 1 hour, or until browned. If desired, sliced cheese may be melted on top during the last 20 minutes of baking.

Vegetable "Patties"

1/4 cup oil
1/2 cup chopped onion
1/2 cup finely chopped celery
1/3 cup peanut butter
1 egg, well beaten
4 Idaho potatoes, cooked, peeled,
 and mashed or diced
1 cup cooked chopped carrots
 or peas
1 1/2 cups flavored bread crumbs
 Oil for frying

In a skillet, heat oil and saute onion and celery until tender (about 5 minutes). Pour into a bowl with the remaining oil. Add peanut butter, potatoes, egg, and vegetables. Stir until well blended. Shape mixture into six patties. Roll patties in crumbs until completely coated. Brown patties on each side in shallow preheated oil (about 350 F) or on greased pan in oven (about 45 minutes). Drain on absorbent paper, if necessary.

VEGETARIAN "CHOPPED LIVER" I

1 very large onion (or 2 medium)
2 tablespoons oil
12 walnuts, grated in a blender
2 cups cooked peas
8 hard-cooked eggs

Saute lightly chopped onion in oil until browned. Mash eggs and add to peas, mixing until well blended. Add walnuts and onions and keep mashing until very well blended.

NUT LOAF

4 tablespoons olive oil
1 cup grated carrots
1 cup chopped celery
1/2 cup chopped onion
1 1/2 cups soya milk
1/4 cup rice polish (or soy flour)
1 teaspoon salt
1 dash pepper (optional)
1/4 teaspoon thyme
1 cup shredded cheddar cheese
1 cup chopped walnuts or pecans
3/4 cup plain wheat germ
3 slightly beaten eggs

Saute in oil, carrots, celery, and onion until tender. Meanwhile, combine in a blender soy milk, rice polish, salt, pepper, and thyme. Pour over the sauted vegetables, cook, and stir over moderate heat until thick. Stir in cheddar cheese, nuts, and wheat germ. For a *pareve* (nondairy) loaf, use shredded firm tofu (soy curd) instead of cheese. Add 3 eggs and mix. Pour into 8x8x2 inch greased baking pan. Bake at 350 F for 40 minutes, or until brown and firm. Let cool a few minutes before slicing. Serve with Pareve Gravy (recipe given later) or onion sauce.

Rice Pudding

1 1/2 cups brown rice
3 cups water
2 beaten eggs (optional)
1 cup raisins (presoaked)
2 grated apples
1 teaspoon cinnamon
apple juice or sesame butter (optional)

Soak brown rice in water overnight. Then cook until soft. Add the remaining ingredients. Put into unwaxed paper bowls (or into muffin cup liners for smaller portions) and bake for 45 minutes at 350 F (or until brown on top).

Millet Pie

1 cup millet
2 1/2 cups water
2 grated zucchini
2 chopped onions
3 tablespoons olive oil
2 beaten eggs
1 teaspoon tamari (soy sauce)

Soak millet in water overnight. Then cook until soft (15-20 minutes). In skillet, saute together zucchini and onions in olive oil. Add soy sauce plus herbal seasoning of your choice. Mix with eggs and bake in oiled 9-inch pie plate for 30 minutes at 350 F.

Eggplant Salad

1 eggplant
1/2 tablespoon olive oil
1/2 tablespoon lemon juice
2 tablespoons plain tahini (unprepared)
1/4 teaspoon salt or soy sauce (optional)

Wash eggplant. Pierce once with knife or fork (to allow heated air to escape when baking) and put in moderate oven for 40 minutes or longer (timing depends on the size of the eggplant). When fully baked, knife will go in very easily. Remove from oven, slit open, and scoop out the pulp. Mash with chopper. When cool, add olive oil, lemon juice, and tahini.

Use your intuition and taste-test for proportions (*any* ratios turn out fine). Serve cold in a scoop on lettuce leaf, or as sandwich filling.

LENTIL SOUP

2 cups lentils
6 cups water
1 small whole onion
2 grated carrots
2 diced potatoes
1 tablespoon chopped celery
2 tablespoons chopped parsley
1/2 teaspoon salt
1/2 teaspoon tamari sauce

Soak washed lentils overnight in water. In the morning, cook with onion, carrots, potatoes, celery, and parsley. Season with salt or tamari (soy sauce). Remove onion before serving.

ZUCCHINI CREAM SOUP

2 diced onions
1 tablespoon sesame oil
6 diced potatoes
4 diced zucchini
2 quarts water
Spike (prepackaged combination of 39 spices, herbs, and flavorings)

Saute onions in oil and set aside. Cook potatoes and zucchini in water until soft. Add Spike or other herbal seasoning and process all the ingredients in the blender until creamy. Serve immediately, with chopped parsley sprinkled on top.

ARTICHOKE

1 artichoke
individual bowls of tahini dressing

Wash artichoke well by running tap water between the leaves. Cook whole (no need to cut or trim) in enough water to cover for about 30 minutes. Serve with tahini for dipping. Artichoke is eaten by tearing off one leaf at a time, dipping it in the tahini, and scraping the leaf between your teeth to extract the edible pulp.

Tahini Dressing

1/2 cup light-colored sesame butter (tahini)
3/4 cup water
1/2 teaspoon Spike
1/4 teaspoon paprika
1/4 teaspoon garlic powder
1/4 teaspoon cumin or curry powder (optional)
1-2 tablespoons oil (optional)

Mix the first four ingredients. You may also add cumin for taste and oil for a creamier texture. Refrigerate and use as dressing over cooked vegetables or as a dip.

Almond Salad Dressing

1/2 cup skinless almonds
1 clove minced garlic
1/2 cup olive oil
juice of 1/2 lemon
1/2 teaspoon salt

Process all the ingredients in a blender. Store and use as needed over salads.

Creamed Zucchini

1 zucchini
1 tablespoon olive oil or 1/4 ripe avocado
chopped fresh dill (optional)
Spike or other seasoning to taste

Wash and trim zucchini. Dice into 1/2-inch pieces and cook in a small amount of water (enough to cover the zucchini) until soft (about 20 minutes). Put half the zucchini (with very little water) into a blender and process with Spike or other seasoning and oil or avocado. Pour mixture into a bowl over the unblended half of the zucchini. Serve cold with dill sprinkled on top.

SPANISH OMELETTE

4 eggs
1/4 teaspoon garlic powder
1/4 teaspoon paprika
1/4 teaspoon salt
1 diced tomato
1/2 diced red or green pepper
2 tablespoons olive oil

In a bowl, beat eggs with fork or whisk, adding the three seasonings as you go. Then add the tomato and pepper and pour mixture in a large skillet in which oil has been preheated. Cook slowly over low flame with the lid on.

CORAL DRESSING

1 diced ripe tomatoe
1 diced half-sour pickle
1/2 cup olive oil

Process all the ingredients in a blender. Use on raw vegetables or over asparagus.

NATURAL SWEETS

YUMMY CUSTARD

5 cups unsweetened apple juice
4 tablespoons agar flakes
4 tablespoons tahini
4 tablespoons arrowroot powder
1 teaspoon vanilla
2 tablespoons carob powder
coconut flakes or chopped pecans

Bring to a boil 4 of the 5 cups apple juice with the agar flakes. Meanwhile, mix in a blender the remaining cup of apple juice, the tahini, and the arrowroot. Add blenderized mixture to boiling mixture and simmer 5 minutes. Add vanilla. For variety, pour half the mixture back into blender, add carob powder, and process. Pour into bowl and let cool. The no-carob half cools separately (take off the stove and set aside). Refrigerate and serve in tall glass goblets, alternating layers of the vanilla and the carob, with a carob swirl on top plus coconut or pecans. Delicious and decorative; a real treat.

Instant Pareve Cheesecake

Crust
1 1/2 cups granola
1/4 cup sesame oil
1 cup toasted slivered almonds
3/4 cup toasted coconut flakes

Filling
2 mashed cakes of firm tofu
1 tablespoon carob powder
1 teaspoon vanilla
1/4 teaspoon cinnamon
3/4 cup honey
1 tablespoon tahini

Mix together all the ingredients for the crust. Press into a 9-inch pie plate. In a large bowl, mix together all the ingredients for the filling. Fill crust, decorate, chill, and serve.

Round Halvah

1/2 cup tahini
1/2 cup finely ground date sugar (powdered dates) or 1/4 cup maple syrup
1/4 cup ground almonds
1 teaspoon vanilla
powdered almonds or coconut flakes

Mix all the ingredients together. Mold into balls, roll in powdered almonds or coconut and refrigerate (can be kept in freezer for long-term storage).

Nice Cream

4 teaspoons raw cashew nuts
4 teaspoons soymilk powder
4 cups unsweetened pineapple juice
4 heaping tablespoons frozen orange juice concentrate
2 ripe bananas
1 cup crushed pineapple or strawberries or peaches

In a blender, process the first three ingredients. Then add orange juice concentrate and reprocess. While blender is running, add fruit. Pour into a container and freeze. Makes 2 quarts.

SNOWBALLS

raisins
apricots (unsulfered)
dates (skinned under warm water and then pitted)
figs
currants
prunes (pitted)
ground nuts (filberts, brazils, or walnuts) (optional)
coconut flakes or ground cashews or almond bean

Put through a food grinder any amount or proportions of the dried fruits. (Add the optional nuts at this time.) Mix well, wet hands, and form 1-inch balls. Roll in coconut, cashews, or almond meal. Store in refrigerator. This is Nature's candy.

NUTTY HEALTH BARS

1 cup toasted oatmeal (pretoast in oven)
1/4 cup ground sesame seeds
1 cup nut pieces (any kind except peanuts)
1/2 cup raw honey
1/4 cup carob powder

Mix the first four ingredients together. Roll out on wax paper, sprinkle with carob powder, and shape into a roll. Refrigerate to harden (wrapped in the wax paper). Slice as needed.

RAW CAKE

1 cup filberts (or any other nut)
1/2 cup apricots, prunes, or other dried fruit
3/4 cup honey
1 cup coconut flakes
1 cup wheat germ
1/4 teaspoon anise or rum or almond extract

Put nuts and dried fruit through a food grinder. Add remaining ingredients, mix, and form into a roll. Wrap in wax paper and refrigerate. Slice as needed.

Tofu Pie

1 cup sunflower seeds, walnuts, and sesame seeds in any proportion
1 1/2 cakes cubed firm tofu (bean curd)
1/2 cup maple syrup
2 eggs
juice of 1/2 lemon
1 teaspoon vanilla
1 peeled, diced apple
2 tablespoons of wheat germ

Grind seeds and nuts in a nut mill. Then press into oiled pie pan to create a "shell." Process the remaining ingredients in a blender, adding the wheat germ only if the mixture is too liquid. Pour blended mixture into pie shell and bake 1 hour at 350 F.

VARIATION: Add whole blueberries to mixture (after pouring into shell) and sprinkle shredded coconut on top.

E-Z Apple Pie

4 peeled, cored, and diced apples
2 beaten eggs
2 teaspoons vanilla
1/2 cup maple syrup
1/3 cup water
3/4 cup whole wheat flour
3/4 cup ground walnuts
2 teaspoons cinnamon (optional)

Mix all the ingredients together. Put into a 9-inch oiled pie plate and bake for 45 minutes at 350 F.

E-Z Peach Pie

4 cups peeded and diced peaches
1 cup maple syrup
2 beaten eggs
1/2 cup sesame or other oil
2 teaspoons vanilla
2 cups whole wheat flour
2 teaspoons baking soda
2 teaspoons Jamaica rum (optional)
1 cup presoaked raisins
1 cup chopped walnuts

Mix all the ingredients together. Pour into oiled pie plate and bake for 45 minutes at 350 F.

C. FESTIVE MEALS

Whether it's for the Sabbath or a holiday, for entertaining quests, or even when you want to treat yourself and your family to a special gourmet meal, there is no limit to the creativity that you can express with foods, without deviating drastically from good nutritional principles. Following are some of my favorite recipes; most of them are printed here for the first time. Enjoy!

SOUPS

MINA'S POTATO SOUP

6 cups water
1 diced potato
1 grated potato
1 grated carrot
1 chopped celery stalk
handful of fresh or dried mushrooms
1/4 teaspoon caraway seeds
salt
pepper

Combine all ingredients and cook until soft.

COOL SUMMER SOUP

2 large cucumbers
salt
2 cups protein broth (from Dr. Bronner's Protein Seasoning)
2 cups plain yogurt
1 tablespoon olive oil
1-2 cloves finely minced garlic
2 tablespoons finely chopped walnuts
2 tablespoons chopped chives or scallion greens
fresh mint

Peel and thinly slice cucumbers. Sprinkle with salt and let stand 20-30 minutes. Prepare protein broth ahead of time and let cool. Mix into yogurt and slowly beat in oil (use hand beater). Rinse cucumber slices and add to yogurt mixture. Add garlic, walnuts and chives and mix well. Refrigerate before serving. Garnish with fresh mint.

Iceberg Soup

1 head of iceberg lettuce
1 large ripe tomato
1 carrot
1 tablespoon olive oil
1 diced onion
1 cup diced mushrooms
1 finely chopped celery stalk
1/2 grated carrot (optional)
Spike or onion and garlic powders or other seasonings

Saute onion and mushrooms together; set aside. Take off a few leaves from a head of iceberg lettuce, slice into noodle shapes, and put aside. Cut the rest of the lettuce into chunks. Put the tomato (cut into chunks) in the blender first and then the lettuce. Use the carrot as a "pusher" and blenderize. Add seasoning. Before serving, mix in the lettuce "noodles," sauted onions and mushrooms, celery, and grated carrot (if desired). Serve cold.

Exodus Kneidlach

(Especially good for Passover)

12 whole wheat matzos
2 finely chopped onions
8 tablespoons olive oil
2 beaten eggs
1 cup warm water
1 teaspoon garlic powder
1 teaspoon salt
finely chopped parsley

Break the matzos by hand and process in blender into matzoh meal (make sure blender container is absolutely dry). Saute onions in half the oil, until transparent, and then set aside. In a separate bowl, beat the eggs with a fork, add the rest of the oil and the warm water. Mix well. Add the garlic powder, salt, and parsley leaves. Mix. Add as much matzoh meal as will be absorbed by the liquid to create a soft dough consistency. Refrigerate for 2 hours. Then form 1-inch balls (wet your palms first) and put them into boiling water or soup. Cook 30 minutes or longer.

SALADS

STUFFED CELERY

celery stalks
Filling
1 tofu cake (1/2 pound)
juice of 1/2 lemon
1 diced dill pickle
1 tablespoon cider vinegar

Process all the filling ingredients in a blender, then stuff the celery stalks.

ISRAELI SALAD

1 ripe finely diced tomato
1/2 chopped green pepper
1 peeled and diced cucumber
2 chopped scallions
2 tablespoons olive oil
2 teaspoons fresh lemon juice
1/4 teaspoon salt

Mix in a cup oil, lemon juice, and salt. Pour over vegetables, toss, and marinate for 30 minutes before serving.

RAINBOW SALAD

carrots, finely grated
raw beets, finely grated
shredded green cabbage

Place equal amounts of carrots, beets, and cabbage in separate bowls. Add a different dressing to each bowl and rearrange in an attractive display on a large serving platter.

Suggested dressings: For the cabbage, Cucumber Dressing (to follow; for the carrots, Pineapple-Raisin Dressing (to follow); for the beets, apple juice.

Cucumber Dressing

1/2 cup peeled, grated cucumber
1/2 cup plain yogurt
1 tablespoon cider vinegar
1 tablespoon honey
1/4 teaspoon salt (optional)
1 teaspoon kelp (optional)
1 mashed, hard-boiled egg
1 teaspoon minced onion
1 teaspoon fresh, finely minced marjoram (presoak if dry)

Put the ingredients in a glass jar, cover, and shake. Use over raw vegetables or mix with shredded green cabbage in Rainbow Salad.

Pineapple-Raisin Dressing

1/2 cup raisins
1 cup water
1 cup pineapple juice (unsweetened canned or fresh)
1/2 cup small chunks pineapple (optional)

Presoak raisins in water for 24 hours. (If you forgot, do the "instant" method of soaking in hot water for 5 minutes.) Mix with pineapple juice and pour over Rainbow Salad. Mix well. Pineapple chunks are an interesting addition.

Main Dishes

Beetburgers

5 medium beet roots
6 cups water
3 beaten eggs
1 cup wheat germ

Boil beet roots in water until semi-soft. Pour off the water draining beets well. Rub the beets under running water to remove the peel. Grate the roots and add the eggs and as much plain wheat germ as it takes to get a good consistency. Form patties and bake in moderate oven for 20 minutes on one side and then turn over for another 15 minutes. Serve plain or with sauce. This recipe is delicious, nutritious, and free of salt or seasoning.

VEGGIE CASSEROLE

1 broccoli
1 cauliflower
3 beaten eggs
1/2 teaspoon garlic powder
1/2 teaspoon paprike
1/2 teaspoon salt
1/2 teaspoon curry powder

Wash broccoli and cauliflower and break into flowerets. Cook or steam for 5 to 6 minutes until semisoft. To the eggs, add the garlic powder, paprike, salt, and curry powder and beat again. Mix eggs and vegetables and put into oiled pan and bake for 15 to 20 minutes in a moderate oven.

ALMOND ROAST

1 cup ground almonds
2 tablespoons vegetable oil
1 teaspoon finely chopped onion
2 cups cooked red beans
2 cups whole wheat bread crumbs
1 finely chopped green pepper
1 teaspoon minced parsley
seasoning to taste (Spike or other)

Mix all the ingredients together and shape into a loaf. Bake for 30 minutes in a moderate oven. Slice after it cools slightly. Top with Pareve Gravy or Onion Sauce (recipes below).

PAREVE GRAVY

4 cups water
1 cup cashews
1 onion cut in chunks
1/4 teaspoon salt
1/2 teaspoon miso (fermented soybean paste)
1/2 teaspoon soy sauce
1 cup chopped mushrooms (optional)
1 tablespoon sesame oil (optional)

Process in a blender the water, cashews, and onion. Put this mixture in a saucepan and bring to a boil, stirring until thick. Turn off heat and add salt, miso and soy sauce to taste. If you decide to add mushrooms, saute them in the oil and then chop fine. Serve over vegetarian roasts, nutburgers, etc.

Onion Sauce

2 tablespoons finely chopped onion
2 tablespoons butter
1 tablespoon rice polish or whole wheat flour
1 1/2 cups water (either tap or leftover from vegetable cooking)
2 teaspoons soy sauce
1/2 teaspoon salt
dash pepper (optional)

Saute onion in butter until light brown. Stir in rice polish or flour and keep stirring until golden color. Pour in water, soy sauce, salt, and pepper. Cook and stir until thickened.

Japanese Spread

2 tablespoons sesame oil
1 large grated carrot
2 chopped onions
1 teaspoon soy sauce
3 teaspoons plain tahini

Saute the carrot and onion in oil. When golden, add soy sauce and plain tahini. Mix and serve on rice cakes as a special treat.

Vegetarian Chopped Liver II

5 chopped medium onions
tablespoon oil
1/2 pound brown lentils (cooked until soft)
5 hard-boiled eggs
1/2 cup walnuts (or other nuts)
1/2 teaspoon Spike or other natural seasoning

Saute onions in oil. Combine all the ingredients and pass through a food grinder. Mix with favorite seasoning. Chill and serve scoops on a bed of lettuce, decorated with tomato slices and stuffed olives.

SHISH KEBAB

- baked potatoes
- steamed yellow squash
- cauliflower
- roasted green peppers
- cooked carrots
- cooked celery (destring before cooking by breaking in half and peeling strings)
- broccoli
- falafel ball (optional)

Cut all ingredients into bite size cubes. String on a wooden or stainless steel skewer any combination of chunks of the ingredients. Roast a few minutes in the oven after wetting with your favorite curry sauce, and serve over brown rice, which is on a bed of lettuce or sprouts. Have more curry sauce on the table for the rice.

GEFILTE DISH

- 2 cakes tofu
- 2 good-sized parsley roots (not parsnip)
- 2 stalks celery
- 2 large onions
- 3/4 cup ground sunflower seeds (raw) (or cashew nuts)
- 3 tablespoons wheat germ
- 2 beaten eggs
- 1 teaspoon salt
- 1 teaspoon honey

Garnish

- 2 sliced onions
- 2 stalks celery (cut in sticks)
- 2 diagonally sliced carrots

Put the tofu, parsley, celery, and onion through a food grinder. Add the remaining ingredients and mix. Put into a clean white cotton cloth (at least 15 inches x 15 inches), form into roll, twist into slight crescent (so it can fit into pot) and then roll up the cotton around it. (For extra security, you may want to put a few stitches with white thread to hold the flap.) Put into a large (wide) stainless steel pot, adding enough salt water to cover the roll, add the garnish, and cook together for about 45 minutes. Lift out the roll onto a flat plate (by lifting up from the bottom with a spatula on one side and supporting the cotton with your hand on the other side, after it has cooled enough). Let cool to room temperature and then refrigerate. Place the sliced carrots and the sticks of celery and some of the liquid in a separate bowl. After 2 hours, or even the next day uncover the roll carefully. Make diagonal 3/4-inch slices with a wide knife or spatula. Place each piece on a plate with a lettuce leaf and decorate with 2 slices of carrot on top. Serve with prepared red horseradish. If the "fish" is dry you can pour a bit of its cooking liquid over it. This is a perfect Shabbat appetizer, to be served cold. Prepare on Friday.

Cholent

1 part red kidney beans
1 part chick peas
1/2 part large white lima beans
1/2 part barley
1/2 part mung beans
2 potatoes (in chunks)
1 or 2 sliced carrots
1 chopped onion
1 or 2 chopped celery stalks
Seasoning: (If 1 part = 1 cup, use 1/2 teaspoon of each spice.) Spike, miso, paprika, cumin

Soak the beans, peas, and barley overnight in enough water to cover. Next morning, cook 1 hour. Then add potatoes, carrots, onion, celery, and lots of seasonings. Mix and cook for 1 more hour. Add a bit of sesame oil, cover and put into 250 F oven for a few hours.

Festive Fruit Platter

Possible color scheme
- Yellow (peaches)
- Black (prunes)
- Yellow (pineapple)
- Red (cherries)
- Orange (apricots)
- Green (honeydew)
- Orange (cantaloupe)
- White (pears)
- Black (raisins)
- White (peeled apple slices)
- Red (watermelon)
- Blue (blueberries)

For a festive fruit meal, organize a multicolored plate of a wide variety of fresh or dried (presoaked, unsulfered) fruits, arranged with contrasting colors and shapes (chunks, balls, sliced, etc.) adjacent to each other to create eye appeal. Use the top of a fresh pineapple (cut across at least 1/2 inch below the stem to create a base) as a decorative centerpiece. Have on hand pitchers of two kinds of dressing: *cashew cream* (blenderize cashew nuts, apple juice plus some dates with their skins rubbed off under warm water and then pitted) and *bananaberry cream* (ripe bananas put through a juicer followed by some red strawberries).

10
Jewish Vegetarian Groups and Activities

Vegetarians are sprouting up all over.
(Slogan on t-shirt)

A. INTERNATIONAL GROUPS

The international center for Jewish vegetarian activities is the Jewish Vegetarian Society. Its headquarters is at *Bet Teva*, 855 Finchley Road, London, N. W. 11 8LX (telephone 01-455-0692). The society has published a quarterly magazine, the *Jewish Vegetarian*, since September 1966. Generally, each issue includes an editorial, articles relating Judaism and vegetarianism, a column about vegetarianism in Israel, announcements of society and related events, book reviews, recipes, and news about the society and its members. Its editor, Philip Pick, has edited *The Tree of Life*, a collection of articles and editorials which appeared in the magazine (see bibliography).

The Jewish Vegetarian Society sponsors many events and activities related to its goals. Its motto, which appears on the masthead of the *Jewish Vegetarian*, comes from Isaiah's prophecy about the future ideal age: "...they shall not hurt nor destroy in all My holy mountain." It has branches in many parts of the world and is currently planning to establish a branch in Jerusalem, its spiritual center. The society publishes and distributes many articles showing the relationship between Judaism and vegetarianism. There are two types of membership available: one for practicing vegetarians, who do not eat flesh foods, and another for nonvegetarians who are in sympathy with the movement.

Because of recent expansions in the Society, in addition to Philip Pick, there are presidents for various regions: Stanley Rubens Le.B of Melbourne Australia is President for the Southern Regions, Rabbi Noach Valley, as discussed in the next section, is President for North America, and Rabbi David Rosen is President for Israel and the East.

The origins of the society show how one person, one letter, one simple act can have a great influence. Philip Pick's daughter, Vivien, wrote a letter about vegetarianism to the *London Jewish Chronicle* in 1965, in which she asked people interested in joining a Jewish vegetarian group to contact her. The response was great, and the result was the Jewish Vegetarian Society.[1]

From its inception in 1966, Philip L. Pick has been the editor of the *Jewish Vegetarian.* He was president of the society for many years and was recently made an honorary life president. He has written many powerful editorials and articles and has spoken at conferences all over the world on the society's goals. He wrote:

> Shall we participate in the use of poisoned carcasses of birds and beasts for food, and ask for a perfect healing? Above all, shall we harden our hearts to the cries of tormented creatures reared in the captivity and darkness of factory farms, and ask for pity and compassion for ourselves and our infants?
>
> Love of humanity, peace, sustenance, and good health, the common birthright of all peoples, cannot be achieved on the basis of the desire for flesh.[2]

B. NORTH AMERICAN GROUPS

The increasingly active Jewish Vegetarians of North America (P.O. Box 1463, Baltimore, MD 21203) is affiliated with the international Jewish Vegetarian Society. It has several hundred members and its current president (1988) is Rabbi Noach Valley, spiritual leader of the Dover Jewish Center, Dover, New Jersey. Rabbi Valley also leads a havurah in his community which frequently has meetings with vegetarian speakers and activities. He recently participated in a panel of clergy discussing connections between various religions and vegetarianism at a conference in Toronto.

The Society publishes a newsletter 4 times a year which is edited by Charles Stahler and Debra Wasserman of Baltimore. The newsletter keeps members informed about Jewish vegetarian activities in various communities and also includes articles, book reviews, and information about Jewish vegetarian contacts. A large number of American rabbis receive the newsletter.

Charles and Debra have been extremely active in planning Jewish vegetarian conferences and in distributing literature at street fairs in various communities. Their diligent efforts have been the glue that has kept the society together functioning actively and creatively.

One of the most active Jewish vegetarians is Jonathan Wolf, who holds many Jewish vegetarian events in his home and at synagogues in Manhattan. He is a committed orthodox Jew, who stresses that all the reasons for being vegetarian have roots in Jewish teachings.

Mr. Wolf periodically teaches a unique course, "Judaism and Vegetarianism" at the Lincoln Square Synagogue in New York. In this course he examines vegetarian values in Jewish sources, compassion for animals, feeding the hungry, ecology, *bal tashchit* ("thou shalt not waste"), and preservation of health. He utilizes material from the Torah and other Jewish sources, modern *responsa*, Jewish legal codes, writings of Rabbi Kook, Joseph Albo, and other Jewish scholars, and fiction by vegetarian authors such as Isaac Bashevis Singer.

The group frequently celebrates the sabbath and Jewish holidays at Jonathan Wolf's home. He recently had about 50 guests for a vegetarian seder. He has been extremely creative in relating vegetarian values to the holidays. Especially interesting is the annual vegetarian *Tu Bishvat* seder, conducted in the tradition of the Kabbalists of Safed (not vegetarians). The seder is conducted with a tasting of samples of the seven species of grains and fruits mentioned in the Bible, accompanied with related readings from the Bible, Talmud, Prophets, and other holy writings, with four special cups of wine.[3] There is much singing, merriment, good feeling, warmth, community, games, and blessings of thanks.

An article about Jonathan Wolf and other American Jewish vegetarians appeared in the *National Jewish Monthly* in April 1976.[4] The article states that there is evidence that the percentage of U. S. Jewish vegetarians is increasing; there has been an increase in interest in vegetarianism at northeastern colleges with large Jewish populations; Camp Ramah, a Jewish camp in Plamer, Massachusetts, has provided a special diet for vegetarians; Jews become vegetarians for a variety of reasons—some are committed *halachic* (Jewish law) vegetarians, but for others, Jewish sources are incidental to their commitment to vegetarianism.

Jewish vegetarian conferences were held at the Vegetarian Hotel in June, 1986 and at Congregation Anshe Chesed in Manhattan in May, 1987. The conferences were well attended and included talks, cooking demonstrations, and planning sessions, along with much socializing and comraderie. Plaques were given for "Jewish Vegetarian of the Year" to Isaac Bashevis Singer in 1986 and to the author of this book in 1987.

Jewish vegetarians were well represented at a 5-day vegetarian conference in Toronto in August, 1987. A special panel was devoted to a discussion of connections between Judaism and vegetarianism. The event was covered by the Canadian Jewish News and by the Canadian Broadcasting System.

Local chapters of the Jewish Vegetarians of North America have become active in many communities in the U. S. and Canada. A listing of contact people and groups is given in the appendix.

Members of the Jewish Vegetarians of North America have been involved in creating and organizing new groups that relate Jewish values to the improvement of conditions for animals:

1. Roberta Kalechofsky is leader of Jews for Animal Rights (JAR). This group attempts to make Jews and others aware of Jewish values related to compassion for animals as contrasted with what they regard as the "unprecedented modern abuse of animals." The group produces literature and post cards related to Jewish teachings on treatment of animals. Further information can be obtained by writing JAR, 255 Humphrey Street, Marblehead, MA 01945, U.S.A.

Roberta has been prolific in producing Jewish vegetarian materials. Through her Micah Press, she has recently published *Haggadah for the Liberated Lamb* and the Sixth Day of Creation (see the bibliography) and has produced a Jewish vegetarian calendar ("the Jewish Vegetarian Year") for 1987-88, which contains many appropriate quotations.

2. Nina Natelson is president and director of CHAI (Concern for Helping Animals in Israel). The group is a non-profit, tax-exempt organization established to assist animal welfare efforts in Israel. CHAI sends necessary veterinary medical supplies to Israel's few, small existing shelters; raises funds to build new shelters in areas where there

are none; makes humane education materials available to children and adults in Israel and provides similar materials based on the Jewish tradition to religious schools in the U.S. CHAI is working to replace the routine strychnine poisoning of animals conducted by municipalities in Israel with humane methods of population control and attitudes of cruelty and indifference with "tsaar ba'alei chayyim", compassion for the suffering of living beings. Further information can be obtained by writing CHAI, P.O. Box 3341, Alexandria, VA 22302 (telephone: (703) 820-1742).

In his inaugural address, Dr. Arthur Green, president of the Reconstructionist Rabbinical College (Church Road and Greenwood Avenue, Wyncote, Pennsylvania 19095), advocated that the Reconstructionist movement appoint a commission to "study the question of vegetarianism, and whether it might not be the proper kashrut for our age." He feels that Reconstructionists could be in the vanguard of those advocating a move toward vegetarianism in the Jewish community to give "authentic Jewish form to the moral passion by which many in our age have been so swayed."

Louis Berman, professor of psychology and staff counselor at the Student Counseling Service, University of Illinois, Chicago Circle, has written a book, *Vegetarianism and Jewish Tradition*, which was published by Ktav in New York. Professor Berman has lectured on vegetarianism in Chicago, New York, Denver, Los Angeles, and Dayton, Ohio, and has taught an evening adult education class in vegetarian cooking in his home town of Evanston, Illinois.

Rabbi Yonassan Gershom, spiritual director of Twin Cities B'nai Or, is an ovo-lacto vegetarian. As an observant Jew and practicing mystic, he sees vegetarianism as an important part of the process of bringing the Messianic Age. Since 1981, his monthly *farbrengen* gatherings in Minneapolis have been vegetarian and chemically free. Reb Gershom also travels widely throughout the U.S., and would be willing to speak at your vegetarian group when in town. He publishes a quarterly newsletter, *Northern Rainbow*, which contains articles and networking resources on practicing holistic Judaism. For further information, contact: Twin Cities B'nai Or, 1915 Park Avenue, Minneapolis, MN 55404. (Telephone: (612) 872-9259)

There is a vegetarian hotel in Woodridge, New York (the Catskills). It was founded in 1920 by its present owner, Fannie Shaffer. It provides a wide variety of kosher food and has lectures and other activities related to vegetarianism, nutrition, and health. Information and directions can be obtained by writing the Vegetarian Hotel at P.O. Box 457, Woodridge, N. Y. 12789 (telephone: (914) 434-4455).

C. VEGETARIANISM IN ISRAEL

Vegetarianism is an active movement in Israel today. It is estimated that there are about 120,000 vegetarians in the country.[5] Because a survey conducted by the army quartermaster corps revealed that 7 percent of all soldiers are vegetarian, the corps is making special efforts to meet their needs. Among other changes, army mess halls now serve a variety of new meat substitutes based on grains, soybeans, and various vegetables, as well as vegetarian dishes such as bourekas, blintzes, and eggrolls filled with potatoes or spinach.[6]

The increasing popularity of vegetarianism in Israel is indicated by the rapid growth of health food stores, from one in 1957 to over 60 in 1984.[7] In addition, most supermarkets and many corner grocery stores carry granolas, whole-wheat flour, brown rice and other natural foods.

There are also a wide variety of vegetarian restaurants in Israel. These include "Back to Nature", "Milk and Honey", "Genesis", "Eternity", and "the Naturalist", all in Tel Aviv, and "Hameshek", "A Bit of the Garden of Eden", "Nevel David (David's Harp)", and the "Bet Anna Ticho", all in Jerusalem.[8]

Amirim is a completely vegetarian community in Israel.[9] It is the only vegetarian-naturalist village without livestock in the world. It is the home of about 60 vegetarian and naturalist families. It is located in the Galilee, near the city of Safed. Its elevation of 600 meters above the Mediterranean Sea and 800 meters above the Sea of Galilee is such that both can be seen from the village. Many families in Amirim provide lodging and meals to vacationers; several have natural food kitchens and other are vegetarian. Vacationers can eat at a variety of homes to sample different types of meals and meet a variety of people. The village store contains a full range of organic foods but no meat, fish or cigarettes. There is a pool and other recreational facilities available for vacationers. Further information may be obtained by contacting M. Stuff, Moshav Amirim, House 22, Bikat Beit Hakarem, Carmel 20115, Israel (telephone: 06-980946).

The former Ashkenazi chief rabbi of Israel, Rabbi Shlomo Goren, the chief rabbi of the Haifa district, Rabbi Shear Yashuv Cohen, and Rabbi Cohen's late father, Rabbi David Cohen (the Nazir) are all vegetarians (see biographies in Chapter 10 for more information about them). These were the first three rabbis to reach the Western Wall after the 1967 war.[10] There have been three vegetarian chief rabbis since the establishment of Israel in 1948.[11]

Mordecai Ben-Porat, a member of the former Rabin (Labour Party) government in Israel, introduced a bill in the Knesset (Israel parliament) that would outlaw flesh eating in Israel.[12] He contends that Israel's hard-pressed economy cannot bear the massive National Health Service costs related to diseases due to the eating of flesh foods. The bill was sent to a special committee for investigation but died when the Labour Party lost the election.

Mr. Ben-Porat also called for a National Obesity Treatment Institute and a halt to the import of beef and other foods rich in animal fat.[13] He claims that an improvement in Israel eating habits could save 4,266 billion Israel pounds and $150 million in foreign currency for food imports.

Replying, then Health Minister Victor Shemtov said that studies have verified that bad eating habits cause "cruel and cumulative clinical effects" in persons between the ages of 40 and 50.[14] In 1975, nearly 7,000 Israelis died of heart disease and diabetes (this constituted 30% of all adult deaths that year) and both diseases, Shemtov states, are "closely associated with faulty food intake and selection."[15]

Mitzpe Hayamim is a health center run on the basis of vegetarian diet and wholistic medical treatment. It has an excellent location on a hill 600 meters above sea level overlooking the Sea of Galilee and the plain of the Jordan Valley. In its serene surroundings and pure mountain air, patients find peace, tranquility, relaxation, and a chance to meditate.[16]

The Seaview Vegetarian Hotel and Health Farm at Rosh Pina has breathtaking views of snowcapped Mount Hermon, the lush Hula Valley, and Sea of Galilee. Many Israelis come there to lose weight, release tension, cure muscular complaints, or just to relax and enjoy.[17] Further information can be obtained from P.O. Box 27, Rosh Pina 12000, Israel (telephone: 06-735409).

As previously mentioned, Philip Pick has been active in setting up a Jewish Vegetarian Society branch in Israel.[18] It held its first public meeting at the Shoresh Hotel in Jerusalem in November 1980. A follow-up meeting was held at the Hebrew Union College in Jerusalem in March, 1981. About 150 enthusiastic people attended and heard talks from Philip Pick and other Jewish vegetarian activists.[19]

The Summer, 1980 issue of the Jewish Vegetarian reported details of initial plans for the Israeli branch of the Jewish Vegetarian Society:

(1) It is proposed that a freehold property in Rahavia, Jerusalem, be purchased.
(2) This would comprise a meeting hall, office, and library for the further promotion in Israel of the Jewish Vegetarian Society's aims.
(3) These facilities would be available to the Israel Vegetarian Union and as an office for the Middle East Region of the International Vegetarian Union.
(4) Rooms fitted with all facilities would be available for permanent or temporary accommodation, preferably, but not exclusively, for retired persons.
(5) The premises could be used for a naturopathic center, for both practice and study.

The International Jewish Vegetarian Society is trying to raise funds to help make this dream a reality.

The first congress of the International Jewish Vegetarian Society was held in Ashkelon in November, 1984. About 120 persons from 11 countries gathered to discuss the society's ideals and plans for future action. They also attended 20 sessions on issues relating Judaism and vegetarianism, featuring such speakers as Philip Pick, Rabbi Shear Yashuv Cohen (chief rabbi of Haifa), and former Minister of the Knesset, Mordecai Ben Porat.

The bi-annual conference of the International Vegetarian Union is scheduled to be held in Israel in 1989. Details may be obtained from Keith Akers, P.O. Box 10238, Arlington, VA 22210.

An article in the December 7, 1985 issue of the Jerusalem Post International Edition, "Vegetarian Paradise", by Martha Meisels, discussed the vegetarian situation in Israel.[20] It pointed out that there are two vegetarian groups there:

1) The Vegetarians and Vegans Movement. They publish a journal *Teva-On* (Nature Strength). Their headquarters is 41 King George Street, Tel Aviv (telephone: 03-299268). They claim to have 1,000 members.

2) The Vegetarians and Vegans Society. They publish a journal *Teva Uvruit* (Nature and Health). Their headquarters is at 25 Sharsheret, Afeka, Tel Aviv, 69 697 (telephone: 03-410143).

There is some difference in philosophy between the two organizations. According to Yehuda Ben-Eliezer, a Society contact person, the Society tends to include vegetarians who joined for moral reasons who are generally more activist, while the older Movement tends to attract vegetarians whose emphasis is on health. Both groups are upset about the high prices for health-foods due to what they regard as discriminatory government subsidies.

Hal and Shelly Cohen have established *Ohr Shalom*, consisting of several children's homes in Israel.[21] When the Cohen's arrived in Israel in 1980 after extensive experience in child care in the U.S., they recognized the great need for an alternative to the traditional child care system for deprived, homeless children. They have provided loving, caring homes within the framework of a "family". Their fourth home, "Friendship House" opened in October 1981 thanks to generous financial help from Philip and Minna Pick and the International Jewish Vegetarian Society.

All the homes are run on vegetarian diets. The Cohens believe that this diet will restore physical health and emotional well being to children who have been neglected for many years. The Cohens hope that *Ohr Shalom*, affiliated with the International Jewish Vegetarian Society, will become a center for spreading vegetarian ideals throughout Israel. Since their stipend from the Israeli Ministry of Welfare covers only half of its operating budget, Orr Shalom depends on tax-deductible donations. Inquiries and contributions can be sent to Hal Cohen, Ohr Shalom Village for Children, P.O. Box 6231, Jerusalem, 91061 Israel.

There are active Jewish Vegetarian Society chapters, affiliated with the International Jewish Vegetarian Society, in Jerusalem, Haifa, and Tel Aviv. Names and addresses of contact people are listed in the appendix.

11

Biographies of Famous Jewish Vegetarians

> I believe that the religion of the future will be based on vegetarianism. As long as people will shed the blood of innocent creatures there can be no peace, no liberty, no harmony between people. Slaughter and justice cannot dwell together.
>
> Isaac Bashevis Singer

In this chapter brief biographies will be given of famous Jews who were vegetarians for all or part of their lives.[1] The author would appreciate hearing about other Jewish vegetarians who have not been included and/ or significant facts that have been omitted from these biographies.

AGNON, SHMUEL YOSEF (1888-1970)

Shmuel Yosef Agnon is a central figure in modern Hebrew fiction. He wrote many novels and short stories about major contemporary spiritual concerns. He won the Israel Prize for Literature in 1954 and 1958 and the Nobel Prize in Literature in 1966, the first time that this honor was given to a Hebrew writer. His folk epic, *The Bridal Canopy*, was widely recognized as one of the cornerstones of modern Hebrew literature.

Agnon was a devout Jew who spent much of his life in Israel. He was extremely devoted to vegetarianism. He wove vegetarian themes into many of his stories, as in the following excerpt:

> He received the Sabbath with sweet song and chanted the hallowing tunefully over raisin wine...The table was well spread with all manner of fruit, beans, greenstuffs and good pies,...but of flesh and fish there was never a sign...The old man and his wife had never tasted flesh since reaching maturity.[2]

Agnon's great sensitivity to all creatures can be seen in the following excerpt from his speech upon receiving the Nobel Prize for Literature:

> Lest I slight any creature, I must also mention the domestic animals, the beasts, and the birds from whom I have learned. Job said long ago (35:11): "Who teacheth us more than the beasts of the earth, and maketh us wiser than the fowls of heaven?" Some of what I have learned from them I have written in my books, but I fear that I have not learned as much as I should have done, for when I hear a dog bark, or a bird twitter, or a cock crow, I do not know whether they are thanking me for all I have told of them or calling me to account.[3]

Cohen, Rabbi David (The NAZIR)

Rabbi Cohen made a major contribution to Jewish vegetarianism by collecting and editing the Jewish vegetarian ideas of Rabbi Kook.[4] He was known as the "Nazir of Jerusalem" because he adopted all the obligations of the Nazarite as described in the Torah; he did not drink wine or cut his hair for a specific period.

He was the father of the present chief rabbi of Haifa, Rabbi Shear Yashuv Cohen, and of the wife of the former Ashkenazi chief rabbi of Israel, Rabbi Goren.

Cohen, Rabbi Shear Yashuv[5]

Rabbi Shear Yashuv Cohen has been a vegetarian from birth and is a patron of the Jewish Vegetarian Society. He was graduated in 1947 from Rabbi Kook's Universal Yeshiva in Jerusalem and was ordained a rabbi by the late Chief Rabbi Herzog. From 1948 to 1953, he was chaplain in the Israeli Defense Forces and chief chaplain of the Israeli Air Forces (1952-53). His many positions include dean of the Harry Fischel Institute for Research in Jewish Law and Seminary for Rabbis and Rabbinical Judges; member of the City Council of Jerusalem (from 1955), deputy mayor of Jerusalem (1965-75); and chief rabbi of Haifa (since 1975).

GORDON, AARON DAVID (1856-1922)

Aaron David Gordon was a Hebrew writer who wrote numerous articles on labor, Zionism, and the Jewish destiny. As a strong advocate of the kibbutz (collective settlement) approach, his writings influenced the Jewish Labor Movement throughout the world. He hoped that kibbutzim would be vegetarian settlements, dependent on the land for their produce.

Gordon believed that Zionism would obtain self-fulfillment through working the land. He came to Israel at the age of 48 and spent many years farming. He saw the state of Israel as a challenge to Jews to make a contribution to humanity. He believed that the Jews would be tested through their attitudes and behavior toward the Arabs.

The importance that Gordon placed on vegetarianism can be seen in the following selection:

> The attitude toward vegetarianism...the attitude toward living creatures is...the clearest test of our attitude towards life and towards the world as it really is...The ethical regard toward living creatures that involves no hope of reward, no utilitarian motive—secret or open, such as honor, shows us...the significance of righteousness and all the other desired traits...righteousness, truth, and the like and eating living creatures!"[6]

GOREN, RABBI SHLOMO (1917-)

Rabbi Shlomo Goren was the Ashkenazic chief rabbi of Israel from 1972. He was formerly the Ashkenazic chief rabbi of Tel Aviv-Jaffa and the chief rabbi of the Israeli Defense Forces. In that capacity, he was the first to conduct a service at the liberated Western Wall in 1967.

Rabbi Goren has written many *responsa* on issues related to modern technology and conditions of modern warfare. He had published a collection of essays on the festivals and holy days. His comprehensive commentary on the section *Berakhot* of the Jerusalem Talmud won the Israel Prize in 1961.

The Rabbi's wife is a life-long vegetarian, having been reared in an orthodox vegetarian home in Jerusalem.[7]

KACYZNE, ALTER (1885-1941)

Alter Kacyzne was born in Lithuania but spent most of his creative years in Warsaw, where many of his plays were success- fully staged. His works include many dramatic poems, ballads, short stories, and one full-length novel, *The Strong and the Weak*, which won much praise for its great historical-political significance. His writing often dealt with people's inhumanity.

Kacyzne became a vegetarian at the age of 18, after a curious dream in which he was forced to eat a roasted child. His vegetarian beliefs were well known in Poland. He and his wife hosted well-attended vegetarian receptions. He was beaten to death with sticks and clubs by Nazis in the Ukraine in 1941 and was buried in a mass grave.[8]

KAFKA, FRANZ (1883-1924)

Franz Kafka was a Czech-born, German novelist whose writing had tremendous influence on western literature and art. His many books include *The Castle*, *The Trial*, and *The Great Wall of China*. His novels have been translated into many languages, including Hebrew, and have been adapted for movies, plays, and operas. The action in his books generally centers around the hero's search for identity.

Kafka was attracted to vegetarianism for health and ethical reasons. While viewing fish at an aquarium, he said, "Now I can look at you in peace; I don't eat you any more." He had little faith in conventional doctors; he was interested in the benefits of nature-cure and raw-foods diets. He was also involved in anti-vivisection activities.[9]

KOOK (sometimes spelled Kuk), RABBI ABRAHAM ISAAC (1865-1935)

Rabbi Abraham Isaac Kook was the first Ashkenazi chief rabbi of Palestine after the British mandate. He was a very prolific writer who helped inspire many people to move toward spiritual paths. He urged religious people to become involved in social questions and efforts to improve the world.

Among Rabbi Kook's many significant writings is "A Vision of Vegetarianism and Peace," in which he gave his philosophy of vegetarianism. As indicated previously, he believed strongly that God wants people to be vegetarian and that meat was permitted as a concession to people's weakness. He thought that the many prohibitions related to the slaughtering and eating of meat were meant as a scolding and reminder that people should have reverence for life; this would eventually bring people back to vegetarianism in the days of the Messiah.[10]

There is a dispute as to whether Rav Kook was a consistent vegetarian.

LEFTWICH, JOSEPH (1892-1984)

Joseph Leftwich was an author, editor, and anthologist. He is considered an authority on Jewish and Yiddish literature. He translated works by Sholom Asch, Max Brod, I. L. Peretz, Zalman Schneur, and Stefan Zweig. He also edited several influential anthologies: *Yisroel, The First Jewish Omnibus* (1933, rev. 1963), a wide selection of Jewish literature from many countries; the *Golden Peacock* (1939), translations for Yiddish poetry; and *The Way We Think* (2 vols., 1969), Yiddish essays in English translation.

Leftwich was an active vegetarian and a patron of the Jewish Vegetarian Society. He wrote brief biographies of vegetarian writers, which appeared in the *Jewish Vegetarian*,[11] and an introduction to *The Tree of Life*, a collection of essays relating Judaism and vegetarianism.

MACCOBY, CHAIM ZUNDEL (THE KAMENITZER MAGGID)[12]

Rabbi Chaim Zundel Maccoby was born in Kamenitz, Russia. He settled in London in 1890 and preached Torah and vegetarianism in the streets of that city. He taught people to have compassion for all living creatures and how to remain healthy with little money. He was known by many as a great and saintly preacher. He was a dedicated vegetarian who wore cloth shoes all year long to show his abhorrence of leather.

In 1975, a Hall of Education Library was opened at Bar Ilan University, Ramat Gan, Israel, dedicated to the memory of the Kamenitzer Maggid.

PERETZ, ISAAC LEIB (1852-1915)

I. L. Peretz was a prolific and versatile writer of Hebrew and Yiddish stories and poems. He was one of the founders of modern Yiddish literature as well as an important figure in Hebrew literature. He had many original ideas and used his rich imagination to champion the cause of the oppressed and common people. His compassion and sensitivity encouraged many aspiring authors. He wrote much about the lives of the chasidim, and the Jewish socialist movement was greatly influenced by his ideas.

RAVITCH, MELECH (1893-1976)[13]

Melech Ravitch was considered the dean of Yiddish poetry. His poems occupy nearly a dozen pages in the Yiddish poetry anthology, *The Golden Peacock* (edited by Joseph Leftwich). He compiled an 850-page anthology of material about Jewish Warsaw called the *Warsaw That Was* and wrote about 200 short portrait sketches of Yiddish writers.

Ravitch's poems and essays expressed universal values. He was a vegetarian most of his life and a patron of the Jewish Vegetarian Society.

ROSEN, RABBI DAVID[14]

Rabbi Rosen was the chief rabbi of Ireland. He received his rabbinic ordination from the Rosh Yeshivah of Ponivez and from Av Bet Din Rabbi Levin. He served as senior minister at the Green and Sea Point Hebrew Congregation in Cape Town, the largest congregation in South

Africa; while there, he opposed the inequities in South Africa.

He, his wife, and two young daughters are ethical vegetarians, which they find completely compatible with orthodox Judaism. Rabbi Rosen feels that vegetarianism is growing among Jews in both South Africa and Ireland, and he is a patron of the Jewish Vegetarian Society. He is in charge of the international anti-deformation campaign of the B'nai B'rith and principal of the Saphir Jewish Heritage Centre in Jerusalem.

SINGER, ISAAC BASHEVIS (1904-)

I. B. Singer was born in Poland but came to the United States in 1935. He has been a writer for the New York Yiddish *Daily Forward* under the pen name of Isaac Warshavsky. His best-selling novels include *The Family Moskat*, *Satan in Goray*, *The Magician of Lublin*, *Gimpel the Fool*, *The Spinoza of Market Street*, and *The Slave*. He won the Nobel Prize for Literature in 1978.

He has been a vegetarian for about 25 years primarily because of compassion for animals, and is a patron of the Jewish Vegetarian Society. He received an award from the Vegetarian Information Service in July 1979 for his contributions to literature and vegetarianism.

The following selection is from Singer's novel, *The Estate*:

> Zadok had begun to worry about another matter: the eating of meat. How could one be opposed to violence and at the same time consume the flesh of innocent beasts and fowl? Could there be a justification for this? It was simply a matter of power. Whoever held the knife slaughtered. But he, after all, was against the rule of might. He had already informed Hannah that he would no longer eat meat, but Hannah had answered him with a lament...She wept, complained, and made such a fuss that Zadok give in to her. He would eat meat, if only she would keep still! But the meat didn't agree with him. Hannah bought giblets, heads, feet, entrails, livers. He felt that he was actually swallowing blood and marrow. It would have been possible to kill him, and cook him, in exactly the same way. How can those who torture creatures talk of justice?[15]

The next excerpt is from his short story, "The Slaughterer":

> Barely three months had passed since Yoineh Meir had become a slaughterer, but the time seemed to stretch endlessly. He felt as though he were immersed in blood and lymph. His ears were beset by the squawking of hens, the crowing of roosters, the gobbling of geese, the lowing of oxen, the mooing and bleating of calves and goats; wings fluttered, claws tapped on the floor. The bodies refused to know any justification or excuse—every body resisted in its own fashion, tried to escape, and seemed to argue with the Creator to its last breath.
>
> And Yoineh Meir's own mind raged with questions. Verily, in order to create the world, the Infinite One had had to shrink His light; there could be no free choice without pain. But since the beasts were not endowed with free choice, why should they have to suffer?[16]

Singer's strong feelings with regard to vegetarianism are indicated in the following selections:

> The longer I am a vegetarian, the more I feel how wrong it is to kill animals and eat them. I think that eating meat or fish is a denial of all ideals, even of all religions. How can we pray to God for mercy if we ourselves have no mercy? How can we speak of right and justice if we take an innocent creature and shed its blood? Every kind of killing seems to me savage and I find no justification for it...[17]
>
> Early in my life I came to the conclusion that there was no basic difference between man and animals. If a man has the heart to cut the throat of a chicken or a calf, there's no reason he should not be willing to cut the throat of a man.
>
> It took me a long time to come to the decision to be a vegetarian because I was always afraid I'd starve to death. But never did I have a moment in these 15 years when I regretted that decision.[18]

12
Summary

> The dietary laws are intended to teach us compassion and lead us gently to vegetarianism.
>
> Rabbi Shlomo Riskin[1]

What a glorious religion Judaism is!

Judaism mandates compassion, not just for Jews, but for the stranger, even for enemies; not just for people, but for all of God's creatures. A person without compassion cannot be considered a descendant of Abraham, our father. Jews are to consider the welfare of animals and to avoid *tsa'ar ba'alei chayim*, inflicting pain on any living creature.

Judaism stresses the preservation of life and health. So important is this that if it might help preserve a life, Jews are commanded to set aside ritual laws related to the Sabbath, *kashrut*, and fasting on Yom Kippur.

Judaism places great emphasis on reducing hunger. A Jew who helps feed a hungry person is considered, in effect, to have fed God. Related to helping the hungry are the important Jewish concepts of pursuing justice, giving charity, being compassionate, and sharing food and other resources.

Judaism teaches that people are to be co-workers with God in preserving and improving the earth. We are to be stewards and to use God's bounties for the benefit of all. Nothing that has value can be wasted or destroyed unnecessarily.

Judaism emphasizes the need to seek and pursue peace. Great is peace for it is God's name, all God's blessings are contained in it, it must be sought even in times of war, and it will be the first blessing brought by the Messiah.

Vegetarianism is the diet most consistent with these important Jewish ideals:

- A vegetarian diet does not require the raising of animals in closed, cramped spaces, where they are denied exercise, fresh air, sunlight, and emotional fulfillment.
- A vegetarian diet is consistent with our body structure and chemistry and is least likely to lead to heart trouble, cancer and other diseases.
- A vegetarian diet does not require the wasting of grain, land, water, pesticide, fertilizer, and fuel while millions die annually from hunger and its effects.
- A vegetarian diet is most consistent with the concepts that "the earth is the Lord's," that we are partners with God in preserving and enhancing the world, and we are not to waste or unnecesarily destroy anything of value.
- A vegetarian diet, by not wasting scarce resources and by not requiring the daily slaughter of helpless creatures of God, is most likely to lead to that day when "nations shall beat their swords into plowshares, their spears into pruning hooks, and not study war any more."

The negative effects of flesh-centered diets are all interconnected: The cruel methods used to raise animals lead to unhealthy animals, which in turn affects human health. The fact that over 80% of all grain grown in the United States is fed to animals contributes to global hunger and energy shortages, both of which lead to greater potential for violence and war; the tremendous amounts of grains grown for animal feed require much fertilizer and pesticides, and their manufacture and use cause extensive air and water pollution and depletion of soil fertility. Waters polluted by pesticides, fertilizers, and other chemicals result in fish that are unhealthy to eat. Finally, wars that result from food and energy shortages have extremely harmful effects on animals as well as people. Everything is connected to everything else.

Vegetarianism, by itself, although an important step in the right direction, is not the complete answer to current critical problems:

- Jews should work to eliminate violations of *tsa'ar ba'alei chayim* related to raising animals for food, scientific testing, the use of animals for furs, and the abuse of animals for sport and entertainment.

- Although a vegetarian diet is a positive step for preserving health, Jews should also work for better health through exercise, elimination of junk foods, and other proper hygiene techniques.
- Jews should work to see that food saved through vegetarian diets gets to hungry people; they should also strive for better social and economic conditions to enable people in poor countries to grow the food that they need for survival.
- In addition to improving the environment through vegetarian diets, Jews should work for better energy, transportation, industrial, and residential systems consistent with the Torah concepts of stewardship and *bal tashchit*.
- Finally, consistent with Torah mandates, Jews should in every way seek and pursue peace by working for more equitable sharing of the earth's resources, more harmonious relations among nations, and a reduction of rapidly increasing arms budgets, which take funds from critical human needs such as education, shelter, employment, health, and proper nutrition.

At the close of this book, one final question will be asked of Jews who plan to continue to eat meat: In view of the strong Jewish mandates to be compassionate to animals, preserve health, help feed the hungry, preserve and protect the environment, and seek and pursue peace and the very negative effects flesh-centered diets have in each of these areas, how do you justify not becoming a vegetarian?

Appendix

A. ACTION-CENTERED IDEAS

This book demonstrates that vegetarianism has many positive benefits—for health, the environment, all God's creatures, and the reduction of world hunger. For those who want to do more to help move the world toward vegetarianism, the following suggestions are provided:

(1) Become well informed. Learn the facts about vegetarianism from this and other books (see the bibliography). Know how to answer questions on vegetarianism, and use such questions to inform others. Of course, relate to others in a patient and positive way.

(2) Spread the word. Wear a button. Put a bumper sticker on your car. Make up posters. Write timely letters to the editor of your local newspapers. Set up programs and discussions. There are a wide variety of interesting vegetarian slogans on buttons, bumper stickers, and T-shirts. For example:

Happiness is reverence for life. Be vegetarian.

Love animals. Don't eat them.

Vegetarianism is good for life.

Use the world vegetarian symbol on correspondence. This will help the vegetarian movement obtain publicity that it badly needs and, because of prohibitive costs, cannot be easily obtained otherwise. Stickers and rubber stamps with the world vegetarian symbol can be obtained from the Jewish Vegetarian Society.

(3) Use the material in this and other vegetarian books in discussions with doctors. Make them aware of the many health benefits of a vegetarian diet.
(4) Ask the rabbi of your synagogue, respectfully, if Jews should avoid eating meat today because of important Jewish principles such as *bal tashchit, tsa'ar ba'alei chayim*, and *pikuach nefesh* that are being violated. Ask if these concepts can be included in sermons and classes.
(5) Request that meat or fish not be served at synagogue and Jewish organizational functions and celebrations, for the reasons presented in this book. Ask school principals and school directors to see that nutritious vegetarian meals are served.
(6) Ask the rabbi and/or head of a Hebrew school to organize a trip to a slaughterhouse so that people can observe how animals are slaughtered. A trip to a factory farm to see how cattle and chickens are raised would also be very instructive.
(7) Try to arrange a synagogue or organizational session where vegetarian dishes are sampled and recipes exchanged.
(8) Speak or organize an event with a guest speaker on the advantages of vegetarianism and how vegetarianism relates to Judaism.
(9) Get vegetarian books into public and synagogue libraries by donating duplicates, requesting that libraries purchase such books, and, if you can afford it, by buying some and donating them.
(10) Work with others to set up a vegetarian food co-op or restaurant or help support such places if they already exist. Encourage people to patronize such establishments.
(11) Register yourself with a community, library, or school speakers'bureau. Become informed and start speaking out.
(12) Contact the food editor of your local newspaper and ask that more vegetarian recipes be printed.
(13) When applicable, to raise awareness, indicate how values of the sabbath and festivals are consistent with vegetarian concepts. For example: Point out that the *kiddush* recited before lunch on the sabbath indicates that animals are also to be able to rest on the sabbath day; on *Sukkot*, note that the *sukkah* (temporary dwelling place) is decorated with pictures and replicas of fruits

and vegetables (never with animal products); on Yom Kippur, observe the mandate expressed in the prophetic reading of Isaiah to "share thy bread with the hungry," which can be carried out best by not having a diet that wastes much land, grain, water, fuel, and fertilizer.

(14) Join the International Jewish Vegetarian Society and a local vegetarian society.

(15) Support groups that are working to reduce world hunger. Some responsible organizations are:

OXFAM-America, 302 Columbus Avenue, Boston, MA 02116
Care, Inc., Tri-State Regional Office, 660 First Avenue, New York, NY 10016
U.S. Committee for UNICEF, 331 E. 38th Street, New York, NY 10016 (note: not associated with UNESCO; supported by Israel)
Project Relief, P.O. Box 1455, Providence, RI 02901
Vegfam, 38 Hampden Road, Walsworth, Hitchin, Herts, SG4 OLD, England (this group's goal is to "feed the hungry without exploiting animals").
Institute for Food and Development Policy (Food First), 2588 Mission St., San Francisco, CA 94110, (415) 648-6090.
American Jewish World Service, 729 Boylston Street, Boston, MA 02116
Jewish Fund for Justice, 1334 G Street, NW, Washington, D.C. 20005
American Friends Service Committee, 15 Rutherford Place, New York, NY 10003
American Joint Distribution Committee, 60 East 42nd Street, New York, NY 10017 (serves mostly Jews overseas)
Mazon, 2288 Westwood Blvd., Los Angeles, CA 90024.

These groups generally go beyond merely providing charitable aid to the needy; they strive, in accordance with Maimonides's concept of the highest form of charity, to make people self-reliant in producing their own food.

(16) If people are not willing to become vegetarians, encourage them to at least make a start by giving up red meat and having one or two meatless meals a week (perhaps Mondays and Thursdays, which were traditional Jewish fast days).

(17) Do not concentrate only on vegetarianism. It is only part of the struggle for justice, compassion, and peace. Become aware and try to affect public policy with regard to the issues raised in this book: not wasting, preserving health, showing compassion for animals, saving human lives, dealing our bread to the hungry, seeking and pursuing peace.

If you feel that problems of world hunger and of convincing people to change their diets are so great that your efforts will have little effect, consider the following:

Our tradition teaches, "It is not for you to complete the task, but neither are you free to desist from it."[1] We must make a start and do whatever we can to improve the world. Judaism teaches that a person is obligated to protest when there is evil and to proceed from protest to action (see Question 9, chapter 7). Each person is to imagine that the world is evenly balanced between the good and the wicked and that his actions can determine the destiny of the entire world, for good or evil.

Even if little is accomplished, trying to make improvements will prevent the hardening of your heart and will affirm that you accept moral responsibility. The very act of consciousness raising is important because it may lead to future changes.

B. HELPING BRING THE MESSIAH TO THE WORLD

Judaism teaches that we are heading toward a kingdom of the Messiah, when "none shall hurt nor destroy in all My holy mountain" (Isa. 11:19). The Jewish tradition asserts that one way to speed the coming of the Messiah is to start practicing the ways that will prevail in the messianic time. For example, the Talmud teaches that if all Jews properly observed two consecutive sabbaths, the Messiah would immediately come.[2] This means symbolically that when all Jews reach the level when they can fully observe the sabbath in terms of devotion to God and compassion for people and animals, the conditions would be such that the messianic period would have arrived.

According to Rabbi Kook and others, based on the prophecy of Isaiah 11 : 6 - 9 (And the wolf shall dwell with the lamb . . ."), the messianic period will be vegetarian. Hence, if all became vegetarian in the proper spirit, with compassion for all animals and human beings, and concern about preserving God's world, perhaps this would mean that the messianic period would be here.

C. THE SERVICE OF THE HEART

Since the destruction of the Temple and the end of animal sacrifices, prayer, the service of the heart, has played a major role in Judaism. The following questions related to vegetarianism should be considered as we prepare for prayer:

Can our prayers for compassion be answered when we do not show compassion for God's defenseless creatures? Can our prayers for sustenance be answered when our eating habits deprive many needy people of a portion of God's bounteous harvests? Can our prayers for good health be answered when we consume flesh with high doses of pesticides, antibiotics, and other chemicals. Can our prayers for rain to nourish our crops be answered when so much of that rain is used to grow feedcrops for animals while the hungry pine away for lack of adequate food and water? Can our prayers for peace (*Sim Shalom*)[3] be answered when we do not share God's provisions, thereby perpetuating war and violence? Can we sincerely chant every sabbath morning "All living things shall praise thee...(*Nishmat Kol Chai T'va'rech Et Shim'Chah*)[4] and have a diet that depends on treating living creatures as machines whose sole purpose is to feed our stomachs?

Are the following words of Isaiah valid today as we fail to show compassion to animals as well as people?

I cannot endure iniquity and solemn assembly;
Your new moons and your appointed feasts,
My soul hates.
They have become a burden to me,
That I am weary to bear.
When you spread forth your hands,
I will hide my eyes from you,
Even though you make many prayers,

I will not listen.
Your hands are full of blood. (Isa 1:12-15)

The following from a poem by Coleridge is also applicable:

He prayeth best who loveth best
all things both great and small
For the dear God who loveth us
He made and loveth all.[5]

The previously told story of Israel Salanter placing compassion for animals ahead of Yom Kippur evening prayers is also relevant.

Rabbi Abraham Joshua Heschel, an outstanding twentieth-century Jewish philosopher, states that more than worship is required by God. "Worship without compassion is worse than self-deception; it is an abomination."[6]

The word "prayer" (*t'filah*) comes from the Hebrew word *l'hit pallel*, which means self-evaluation. Our self-evaluation could be enhanced if we acted with compassion toward hungry people and defenseless creatures.

D. IMITATION OF GOD

The Jewish tradition asserts that we are to imitate God's actions. This is related to the biblical account of the creation of man in the image of God (Gen. 1:26). Other biblical sources for the commandment to imitate God are found in the statement that we are to be holy as God is holy (Lev. 19:2) and that we are to walk in God's ways. (Deut. 10:12).

A rabbinic statement that we should imitate God is that of Hama bar Hanina in his commentary on the verse, "After the Lord your God ye shall walk" (Deut. 13:5):

> How can man walk after God? Is He not a consuming fire? What is meant is that man ought to walk after (imitate) the attributes of God. Just as the Lord clothes the naked, so you shall clothe the naked. Just as He visits the sick, so you shall visit the sick. Just as the Lord comforted the bereaved, so you shall also comfort the bereaved; just as He buried the dead, so you shall bury the dead.[7]

The rabbis stress that Jews are to imitate God's qualities of kindness, compassion, and forbearance; however, they do not advise that we imitate God in His infrequent attribute of harsh justice.

As the Lord is our shepherd, we are shepherds of voiceless beasts. As God is kind and compassionate to us, we should be considerate of animals.

By showing compassion to animals through a vegetarian diet, we help fulfill the commandment to imitate God's ways.

E. OUR WEDDING VOW TO GOD

The Prophet Hosea states that we have, in effect, a wedding vow to God. What are the conditions of our betrothal?

> *I will betroth you unto me forever;*
> *I will betroth you unto me in righteousness*
> *and in justice, in loving kindness and in*
> *compassion. I will betroth you unto me in*
> *faithfulness, and you shall know the Lord.*
>
> (Hos: 2:21-2)

Orthodox Jews recite these words every weekday morning as they wrap the *tefillin* strap around their fingers as a symbolic wedding ring.

This wedding vow echoes and reinforces much of what we have said elsewhere in this book. We are wed to God; we are to be co-workers, and the traits that we are to exhibit are righteousness, justice, loving-kindness, and compassion. These important traits, which constitute our wedding vow to God, are echoed in other statements of the prophets:

> *What does the Lord require of you*
> *but that you act justly,*
> *love kindness,*
> *and walk humbly with thy God.* (Mic. 6:8)

> *Thus sayeth the Lord,*
> *"Let not the wise man glory in his wisdom,*
> *Let not the mighty man glory in his might,*
> *Let not the rich man glory in his riches,*
> *but let him who glories, glory in this,*

That he understands and knows me,
That I am the Lord,
Who practices kindness, justice, and righteousness,
in the earth,
For in these things I delight,"
sayeth the Lord. (Jer. 9:22-23).

It is not enough just to know that there is a God but to know and imitate his ways, which involve kindness, justice, and righteousness.

These characteristics are all consistent with vegetarian diets:

We work for righteousness when we eat in such a way that there is no violence toward either man or beast.

We work for justice when our diets are such that all can get their just share of God's bountiful harvests.

We show loving-kindness to all people when our diets enable them to lead a properly nourished life.

We show compassion for animals when our diets do not require their mistreatment and slaughter.

F. JEWISH VEGETARIAN CONTACTS

For an updated list, contact the Jewish Vegetarians of North America, P.O. Box 1463, Baltimore, MD 21203.

CANADA - Evelyn Dorfman, JVS, #22 Shaelborne Avenue, Toronto, Ontario M5N 1Y7, (416) 785-0677.

CALIFORNIA - Marvin Kaufman, A. Goldman, AJVS, PO 38281, LA, CA 90038. (213) 468-5121 or 203-9376; Eugene Gendel, Ph.D., 7806 Turbo Street, Long Beach, CA 90808 (213) 598-4149.

DELAWARE - Ann Zweigle, 940 Buck Drive, Dover, DE 19901. (302) 734-8976.

FLORIDA - Richard Berman D.C., 7760 Country Place, Goldenrod Villas, Winter Pk., FL. 32792. (305) 678-2459. Samuel Shaffe, P.O. Box 9033, Winter Haven, FL 33883. (813) 299-5370. Bess Lemberg, 2704 Woodring Drive, Clearwater, FL 33519. (813) 791-3471. (Call about events.)

GEORGIA - Laura Vendeland, 2418 E. Dunwoody Crossing, Atlanta, GA 30338

HAWAII - Phyllis Canete, 46-355 Holopu Place, Kaneohe, Oahu, HI 96744.

IOWA - Norty Wheeler, Bldg. 1, #118, 2300 Indian Mills Drive, Sioux City, IA 51104.

ILLINOIS - Dr. Louis Berman, Student Counseling Services, University of Illinois, Chicago, IL 60680.

MARYLAND - Charles Stahler and Debra Wasserman, Jewish Vegetarians of North America, PO 1463, Baltimore, MD 21203. (301) 752-VEGV

MASSACHUSETTS - Roberta Kalechofsky, Jews for Animal Rights (JAR), 255 Humphrey St., Marblehead, MA 01945 (617) 631-7601.

MINNESOTA - Rabbi Yonassan Gershom, 1915 Park Avenue South, Minneapolis, MN 55404 ((612) 872-9259).

MISSOURI - Dr. Glen and Sandra Hausfater, 1416 Bradford Dr., Columbia, MO 65203 (314) 874-0847.

MONTANA - Deinya Maichen, 426 4th Ave., Great Falls, MT 59401.

NEW JERSEY - Rabbi Noach Valley, 43 Dogwood Trail, Randolph, NJ 07869. (201) 361-2257. (Has monthly meetings except in the summer.) Ruth Pilichowski, 8-10 Park Ave., Fair Lawn, NJ 07410. (201) 797-2235.

NEW HAMPSHIRE - Philip Paskowitz, Bldg. 6, Apt. 2, 203 Loudon Rd., Concord, NH 03301.

NEW YORK - Richard Schwartz, Sunnyside Campus, CUNY (#H-7), Staten Island, NY 10301; S. Judah Grosberg, Box 144, Hurleyville, NY 12747; J. Grauer, 532 5th St., E. Northport, NY 11731 (516) 757-8990; Jonathan Wolf, #1E, 210 Riverside Dr., NYC 10025, (212) 666-6216; For events call Asher (212) 496-6385, Herb (516) 496-3541, Yael (212) 582-4619. QUEENS VEGETARIAN SOCIETY - F. Mitrani, 54-18 Kissena Blvd., Flushing, NY 11355; Monroe Burton, Chiropractor, 24 E. Stanton Ave., Baldwin, NY 11510 (516) 223-0801; Rabbi Michael Robinson, Temple Israel, Glengary Road, Croton-on-Hudson, NY 10520.

NORTH CAROLINA - N.C. J.V.S, 1310 LeClair St., Chapel Hill, NC 27514 (Has meetings.) Rabbi Robert A. Seigel, Temple Beth El V'Shalom, 1727 Providence Road, Charlotte, NC 28207 (704) 366-1948.

OHIO - Elliott and Sharon Frankenthal Zinner, 23249 S. Woodland Road, Shaker Heights, OH 44122, (216) 751-7991.

PENNSYLVANIA - Leo and Ruth Levi (215) 567-2176; Phil Becker (215) 356-2746; Ellen Sue Spivack, 524 Rural Avenue, Williamsport, PA 17701.

TENNESSEE - Anna Olswanger, 6717 Wind Mill Lane, #1, Memphis, TN 38119.
VIRGINIA - Rabbi Abe Raich, 118 O'Canoe Place, Hampton, VA 23661.
WISCONSIN - Debbie Friedman, 18 Chippewa Ct., Madison, WI 53711.
ENGLAND - THE JEWISH VEGETARIAN SOCIETY Bet Teva, 855 Finchley Road, London, England NW11 8LX.
ISRAEL - Alter Ohrenstein, Box 4190, Haifa 31041. Hal Cohen, J.V.S., JERUSALEM CHAPTER, Ohr Shalom, Box 6231, Jerusalem, Israel 91061. (Ohr Shalom runs a program for neglected and abused children). Jonathan Danilowitz, 12 Ben Gurion Blvd., 63454 Tel Aviv. (Concern for Helping Animals in Israel), Nina Natelson, Box 3341, Alex., VA 22302. (703) 820-1742.

Notes

Chapter 1. *A Vegetarian View of the Bible*

1. Rashi's commentary on Genesis 1:29.
2. Quoted in Nechama Leibowitz, *Studies in Bereshit (Genesis)* (Jerusalem: World Zionist Organization (3rd Edition), 1976), p. 77.
3. Sanhedrin 59b.
4. Quoted by Rabbi Alfred Cohen, "Vegetarianism from a Jewish Perspective," *Journal of Halacha and Contemporary Society*, Vol. I, No. II, (Fall, 1981), p. 45.
5. Joseph Albo, Sefer ha-Ikkarim, Vol. III., Chapter 15.
6. Rabbi J. H. Hertz, *The Pentateuch and Haftorahs* (London: Soncino Press, 1958), p. 5.
7. This view was shared by I.B. Levinson, an early Jewish vegetarian writer. *The Jewish Encyclopedia*, vol. 12 (New York: Ktav), p. 405.
8. Arlene Groner, "The Greening of Kashrut—Can Vegetarianism Become the Ultimate Dietary Law?" *The National Jewish Monthly* (April, 1976), p. 13. Also see "*Afikim baNegev*," in *HaPeles* (Berlin), 1903-4 and "*Talele Orot*," in *Takhkemoni* (Berne), 1910.
9. Quoted by P. Pick, "The Source of Our Inspiration" (Jewish Vegetarian Society paper, London), p. 2.
10. Rabbi Samuel H. Dresner, *The Jewish Dietary Laws, Their Meaning for Our Time* (New York: Burning Bush Press, 1959), pp. 21-25; Cassuto, commentary on Genesis 1:27.
11. Groner, "The Greening of Kashrut", p. 13.
12. Leibowitz, *Studies in Bereshit*, p. 77.
13. Rabbi Isaak Hebenstreit, *Graves of Lust* (Hebrew), (Rzeszow, Poland, 1929), p. 6.
14. Samson Raphael Hirsch's commentary on Genesis 9:2.
15. Dresner, *The Jewish Dietary Laws*, p. 29.

16. Quoted by Leibowitz, *Studies in Bereshit*, p. 77.
17. Hertz, *Pentateuch and Haftorahs*, p. 32.
18. This speculation is considered by Pick, "The Source of Our Inspiration," p. 3.
19. See Rabbi Elijah J. Schochet, *Animal Life in Jewish Tradition* (New York: Klav), 1984, p. 290; also see S. Clayman, "Vegetarianism, The Ideal of the Bible," *The Jewish Vegetarian* (Summer, 1967): 136-137, and Hebenstreit, *Kivrot Hata'avah*, p. 7.
20. Hertz, *Pentateuch and Haftorahs*, p. 276.
21. Talmudic sage Ben Zoma taught as follows: "Who is rich? The person who rejoices in his or her portion" (Pirke Avot 4:1).
22. Reverend A. Cohen, *The Teaching of Maimonides* (New York: Bloch Publishing Co., 1927), p. 180.
23. *Encyclopedia Judaica*, Vol. II, p. 1152.
24. Schochet, Animal Life, p. 300.
25. Rabbi J. David Bleich, "Vegetarianism and Judaism", *Tradition*, Vol. 23, No. 1, (Summer, 1987), p. 86.
26. Ibid., p. 87.
27. Hebenstreit, *Kivrot Hata'avah*, p. 9.
28. Chulin 84a.
29. Pesachim 49b.
30. See the discussion in Joe Green, "Chalutzim of the Messiah—The Religious Vegetarian Concept as Expounded by Rabbi Kook", p. 2.
31. Ibid., pp. 2-3.
32. Rabbi Abraham Isaac Kook, "Fragments of Light," in *Abraham Isaac Kook*, ed. and trans. Ben Zion Bokser (New York: Paulist Press, 1978), pp. 316-21.
33. Quoted in Abraham Chill, *The Commandments and Their Rationale*, (New York, 1974), p. 400.
34. Rabbi Pinchas Peli, *Torah Today* (Washington, D.C.: B'nai B'rith Books, 1987), p. 118.
35. Cohen, "Vegetarianism...", p. 45; Groner, "Greening of Kashrut", p. 13.
36. *Olat Rayah*, Vol. I, p. 292. Cited by Cohen, "Vegetarianism...", p. 45.
37. Rabbi Abraham Isaac Kook, *A Vision of Vegetarianism and Peace*.
38. Hertz, *Pentateuch and Haftorahs*, p. 5.

39. Green, "Chalutzim of the Messiah," p. 1.

CHAPTER 2. Tsa'ar Ba'alei Chayim—*Judaism and Compassion for Animals*

1. Shabbat 77b
2. Maimonides, *Guide of the Perplexed*, 3:17.
3. Sefer Hasidim (ed. Reuben Margolies), No. 666.
4. Baba Metzia 32b; Shabbat 128b.
5. Rabbi Solomon Ganzfried, *Code of Jewish Law* (New York: Hebrew Publishing Co., 1961), book 4, chapter 191, p. 84.
6. Rabbi Samson Raphael Hirsch, *Horeb*, Dayan Dr. I. Grunfeld, trans. (London: Soncino Press, 1962), vol. 2, p. 293.
7. Choshen Mishpat 338.
8. Hirsch, *Horeb*, p. 293.
9. Rashi's commentary on Deuteronomy 25:4.
10. Hertz, *Pentateuch and Haftorahs*, p. 854.
11. William E. H. Lecky, *History of European Morals*, 3rd ed. rev. (New York: Appleton-Century-Crofts, 1903), vol. 2, p. 162.
12. Kilayim 8:2-3; Baba Metzia 90b.
13. Shulchan Aruch, Yoreh De'ah 297:2.
14. Hirsch, *Horeb*, p. 287.
15. Gittin 62a; Berachot 40a.
16. Yerushalmi Ketuvot 4:8 and Yevamot 15:3.
17. Shulchan Aruch, Orach Chayim 167:6; Berachot 40a.
18. Rashi's commentary on Exodus 23:12.
19. Hertz, *Pentateuch and Haftorahs*, p. 298.
20. Maimonides, *Guide of the Perplexed*, 3:48.
21. Ibid.
22. Ibid.
23. Ibid.
24. Rabbi E. J. Schochet, *Animal Life in Jewish Tradition*, (New York: Ktav, 1984), p. 216.
25. Abraham Chill, *The Commandments and Their Rationale* (New York, 1974), p. 114.
26. Ibid.
27. Abot de R. Nathan, chapter 23.

28. Shabbat 128b; Bava Metzia 32b.
29. Encyclopedia Judaica 8:1111.
30. Avodah Zorah 18b.
31. Yorah Deah, Second Series, 10.
32. Shochet, *Animal Life*, pg. 283-287.
33. Joe Green, *The Jewish Vegetarian Tradition* (Johannesburg, South Africa: Joe Green, 1969), p. 15, based on the teaching of the Ramah.
34. Dresner, *Jewish Dietary Law*, pp. 33-34.
35. Shulchan Aruch, Orach Chayim 223:6.
36. Ganzfried, comp. *Code of Jewish Law*, vol. 2, p. 29.
37. Shabbat 128b.
38. Shulchan Aruch, Orach Chayim 316:2.
39. Shulchan Aruch, Orach Chayim 332:2.
40. Shulchan Aruch, Orach Chayim 332:3.
41. Shulchan Aruch, Orach Chayim 332:4.
42. Shulchan Aruch, Orach Chayim 305:19.
43. Quoted by Aviva Cantor, "Kindness to Animals", in the *Third Jewish Catalog* (Philadelphia: The Jewish Publication Society of America, 1980), p. 289.
44. Exodus Rabbah 2:2.
45. Tanchuma, Noah 3; cited by Schochet, Animal Life, p. 148. Joseph was also considered a tzadik because of his resistance to sexual temptations.
46. Genesis Rabbah, Noah 31:14.
47. Baba Metzia 85a; Genesis Rabbah 33:3.
48. Noah J. Cohen, *Tsa'ar Ba'ale Hayim—The Prevention of Cruelty to Animals, Its Bases, Development and Legislation in Hebrew Literature* (Jerusalem: Feldheim, 1976), pp.4-5.
49. Ibid.
50. Rabbi Alfred Cohen, "Vegetarianism from a Jewish Perspective", *The Journal of Halacha and Contemporary Society*, Vol. I., No. II, (Fall, 1981), p. 48.
51. S. Y. Agnon, *Days of Awe* (Jerusalem: Shocken, 1939.)
52. Martin Buber, *Tales of the Hasidim*, vol. 1, p. 249.
53. Mordecai Ben Ammi (1854-1932), quoted by Joe Green, *The Jewish Vegetarian Tradition*, pp. 19-20.
54. Schochet, *Animal Life*, p. 47.
55. A detailed treatment of how chickens are raised under factory

conditions is given by Peter Singer, *Animal Liberation* (New York: Avon Books, 1975), pp. 99-103.

56. Ruth Harrison, *Animal Machines* (London: Vincent Street, 1964), pp. 54-55.

57. "Pets or Pate," *The Jewish Vegetarian* 23 (Spring, 1972): 7-8.

58. "Fois Gras from Israel Vies With The French", *New York Times*, Sept. 10, 1980.

59. Rabbi A. Spero, "An Update on White Veal and its Halachic Implications", *The Jewish Press*, Oct. 8, 1982, p. 27, and Oct. 15, 1982, p. 19.

60. Nathaniel Altman, *Eating for Life* (Wheaton, Ill.: Theosophical Publishing House, 1977), pp. 76-77.

61. R. Harrison, p. 12.

62. John Harris, "Killing for Food," in *Animals, Men, and Morals*, S & R Godlovitch and John Harris, eds. (New York: Taplinger Publishing Co., 1972), p. 98.

63. Harrison, *Animal Machines*, p. 3.

64. R. Ezekiel Landau, *Teshuvot Noda bi-Yehudah, Mahadura Kamma Yoreh De'ah*, No. 83.

Chapter 3. *Preserving Health and Life*

1. Rabbi Samson Raphael Hirsch, *Horeb*, Dayan Dr. I. Grunfeld, trans. (London: Soncino Press, 1962), pp. 299-300.

2. Chulin 9a; Choshen Mishpat 427; Yoreh De'ah 116.

3. Pesachim 25a; Maimonides, Yad, Yesode ha Torah, p. 7.

4. Yoma 85b; Sanhedren 74a.

5. Rabbi J. H. Hirsch, *The Pentateuch and Haftorahs* (London: Soncino Press, 1958), p. 843.

6. Ibid.

7. Maimonides, *Hilchot Rotze'ach*, chapter 11, part 4.

8. Fred Rosner, *Modern Medicine and Jewish Law* (New York: Bloch, 1972), p. 28.

9. Ibid.

10. Ta'anit 20b.

11. Sanhedrin 4:5

12. Shabbat 151b

13. Sefer Hasidim, #724
14. Ta'anit 11a, b.
15. Shabbat 140b.
16. Chulin 84a; Avodah Zarah 11a.
17. Shabbat 50b.
18. Leviticus Rabbah 34:3.
19. Rosner, *Modern Medicine*, p. 30.
20. Hirsch, *Horeb*, pp. 299-300
21. Ibid, p. 31.
22. Mikkel Hindhede, *American Journal of Epidemiology* 100, no. 5:394.
23. Nathaniel Altman, *Eating for Life* (Wheaton, Ill.: Theosophical Publishing House, 1977), p. 22.
24. John A. Scharffenberg, *Problems with Meat* (Santa Barbara, Calif.: Wadsworth, 1977), p. 28.
25. Ibid.
26. R. L. Phillips, "Role of Lifestyle and Dietary Habits in Risk of Cancer among Seventh Day Adventists," *Cancer Research* 35 (November 1975): 3513.
27. Morton Mintz, "Fat Intake Increasing Cancer Risk," *Washington Post*, September 10, 1976.
28. B. Armstrong et al., "Blood Pressure in Seventh Day Adventists," *American Journal of Epidemiology* 105, no. 5 (May 1977): 444-9.
29. Ibid.
30. Gene Marine and Judith Van Allen, *Food Pollution: The Violation of Our Inner Ecology* (New York: Holt, Rinehart and Winston, 1972), p. 19.
31. Paul Dudley White, *American Heart Journal* (December 1964): 842.
32. Harold Habenicht, "The Vegetarian Advantage," *The Vegetarian Way, Proceedings of the 24th World Vegetarian Conference*, Madras, India (1977), p. 23.
33. "Hold the Eggs and Butter", *Time* (March 26, 1984): pp. 56-63.
34. Connor, W. "The Key Role of Nutritional Factors in the Prevention of Coronary Heart Disease." *Preventive Medicine*, Vol. 1, 1979, p. 49; "Facts of Vegetarianism," North American Vegetarian Society, Malaga, N.J., p. 7.
35. W. S. Collens, "Arteriosclerotic Disease, An Anthropologic The-

ory," *Medical Counterpoint* (December 1969): 55.

36. "Report of Inter-Society Commission for Heart Diseases," *Circulation* 42 (December 1970): A53-95.

37. Senate Select Committee on Nutrition and Human Needs, *Dietary Goals for the United States* (Washington, D.C.: U.S. Government Printing Office, 1977).

38. Scharffenberg, *Problems with Meat*, p. 29.

39. "Nutritionist Nathan Pritikin says average Jewish diet 'must have been designed by enemies of Jewish people'", *Canadian Jewish News*, June 26, 1980.

40. Letter, The American Institute for Cancer Research, Washington, D.C. 20070.

41. Ernest L. Wydner, *Cancer Research* (November 1975): 3238.

42. Victor Sussman, *The Vegetarian Alternative* (Emmaus, Pa.: Rodale Press, 1978), p. 60.

43. Ibid.

44. Broitman, Selwyn A., Ph.D., *et al.* "Polyunsaturated Fat, Cholesterol and Large Bowel Tumorigenesis." *Cancer*, Vol. 40, Nov. 1977, p. 2455; Cruse, Peter, *et al.* "Dietary Cholesteral is Cocarcinogen for Human Colon Cancer." *Lancet*, Vol. I, April 7, 1979, p. 752; sources cited by Marilyn and Harvey Diamond, *Living Health*, (New York: Warner Books, 1987), p. 220.

45. Hill, M. "Colon Cancer: A Disease of Fiber Depletion or of Dietary Excess." *Digestion*, Vol. II, 1974, p. 289; Reddy, Bandaru S., Ph.D., et al. "Metabolic Epidemiology of Large Bowel Cancer." *Cancer*, Vol. 42, Dec. 1978, p. 2832; sources cited by Diamond, *Health*, p. 220.

46. Frey Ellis, *The Jewish Vegetarian* 35 (April 1975): 37.

47. Ibid.

48. John Henry Kellogg, *The New Dietetics* (Modern Medicine Publishing Co., 1927), p. 870.

49. Ibid.

50. "Doctors say special diet can aid kidney patients", *Staten Island Advance*, Sept. 6, 1984.

51. Dudley Giehl, *Vegetarianism: A Way of Life* (New York: Harper and Row, 1979), p. 30.

52. Habenicht, "The Vegetarian Advantage," p. 27.

53. "Facts of Vegetarianism," p. 5.

54. Ibid.

55. M. M. Bhamgara, "Yoga and Diet," *The Vegetarian Way, Proceedings of the 24th World Vegetarian Congress*, Madras, India (1977): 137.

56. Barbara Parham, *What's Wrong with Eating Meat*? (Denver, Colo.: Ananda Marga Publications, 1979), pp. 10-11.

57. R. H. Wheldon, *No Animal Food* (New York: Health Culture Co.), p. 50, quoted by Altman, *Eating for Life*, p. 17.

58. Rachel Carson, Foreword, in Ruth Harrison, *Animal Machines* (London: Vincent Street, 1964).

59. T. Netweit, "Why Do I As a Veterinary Surgeon Prefer Vegetarian Food?," *The Jewish Vegetarian* 42 (August 1977), p. 19.

60. Habenicht, "The Vegetarian Advantage," p. 25.

61. Quoted by Parham, *What's Wrong with Eating Meat*?, pp. 15-16.

62. Netweit, "Why Do I?" pp. 18-19.

63. Karen Pryor, *Nursing Your Baby* (New York: Harper and Row, 1963), p. 65.

64. Available from the Environmental Defense Fund, 1525 18 Street, N.W., Washington, D.C. 20036.

65. Sussman, *Vegetarian Alternative*, p. 41.

66. "Antibiotic Feed Additives: The Prospect of Doing Without", *Farmline*, U.S. Dept. of Agriculture, Dec., 1980.

67. Ibid.

68. "Farm feed antibiotics pose threat", *Staten Island Advance*, June 25, 1979.

69. "Faster chicken production lines has the inspectors squawking", *Staten Island Advance*, Oct. 4, 1979, p. 6.

70. Rabbi Alfred Cohen, "Vegetarianism from a Jewish Perspective", *Journal of Halacha and Contemporary Society*, Vol. I, No. II, (Fall, 1981), p. 61.

Chapter 4. *Feeding the Hungry*

1. Testimony before the Ad Hoc Senate Committee on World Hunger.

2. Baba Batra 9a.

3. Midrash Tannaim.

4. *Passover Hagaddah.*

5. "World Hunger Facts," p. 2. This is available at Oxfam America's Facts for Action, 115 Broadway, Boston, MA 02116, p. 2.
6. Ibid.
7. Ibid.
8. Ibid.
9. "1981 World Population Data Sheet," Population Reference Bureau, Washington, D.C.
10. Pablo Neruda, excerpt from *The Great Tablecloth*, quoted in "World Hunger Facts."
11. *Philadelphia Inquirer*, 13 Oct. 1974, p. 9B.
12. Lester R. Brown, *In the Human Interest* (New York: Norton, 1974), p. 21.
13. A detailed analysis of the waste related to livestock agriculture is in *Diet For a Small Planet* by Frances M. Lappe, Tenth Anniversary Issue (New York: Ballantine, 1972).
14. Georg Borgstrom, *The Food and People Dilemma* (Belmont, Calif.: Wadsworth, 1973), p. 63.
15. Georg Borgstrom, "Present Food Production and the World Food Crisis," paper presented on September 2, 1974.
16. *New York Times*, July 22, 1975, p. 8.
17. *Food First Resource Guide* (San Francisco: Staff of the Institute for Food and Development Policy), 1979, p. 7.
18. Quoted by Philip Nobile and John Deedy, *The Complete Ecology Fact Book* (Garden City, N.Y.: Doubleday, 1972), p. 277.
19. James Parsons, "Forest to Pasture: Development or Destruction?" *Revista de Biologia Tropical*, vol. 24, supplement 1, 1976, p. 124, cited by Frances M. Lappe, *Diet For a Small Planet*, (New York: Ballantine, 1982), Tenth Anniversary Edition, p. 63.
20. Ibid.
21. Robin Hur, *Food Reform: The Desparate Need* (Austin, Texas: Heidelberg, 1975), p. 188.
22. Rabbi Emanuel Rackman, "Torah Concept of Empathic Justice Can Bring Peace," *The Jewish Week* (April 3, 1977): 19.
23. Ibid.
24. Ketubot 68a.
25. Maimonides, *Yad*, Hilchot Matnot Aniyim 7:10.
26. Maimonides, *Mishneh Torah*, Hilchot Matnot Aniyim 10:7.
27. Shabbat 63a.

28. Exodus Rabbah, Mishpatim 31:14.
29. Pirke Avot 3:21.
30. Betza 32a.
31. Eruvim 41.
32. Nedarim 64b.
33. Gen. 18:2; Abot de Rabbi Nathan 7:17a,b.
34. Maimonides, *Yad Hazakam* Hilchot Shabbat 2:3.
35. Bezah, 32b.
36. Yebamot 79a; Numbers Rabbah 8:4.
37. Rashi's commentary on Genesis 41:50, based on Ta'anit 11a.
38. Rabbi Samson Raphael Hirsch, *Horeb*, Dayan Dr. I. Grunfeld, trans. (London: Soncino Press, 1962), vol. 1, pp. 54-55.
39. Pirke Avot 1:14.
40. Berachot 55a.
41. Paper on world hunger put out by Morzone, ad hoc Jewish group on hunger.
42. Class before *Pesach* given at Young Israel of Staten Island, attended by author.
43. Jay Dinshah, *The Vegetarian Way, Proceedings of the 24th World Vegetarian Conference*, Madras, India (1977): 34.
44. "The Energy-Food Crisis: A Challenge to Peace—A Call to Faith," a statement from the Interreligious Peach Colloquium held in Bellagio, Italy, May 1975.
45. Ronald J. Sider, *Rich Christians in an Age of Hunger* (Downers Grove, Ill.: Intervarsity Press, 1977), p. 25.
46. Boyce Rensberger, "World Food Crisis: Basic Ways of Life Face Upheaval from Chronic Shortages," *New York Times*, November 5, 1974, p. 14.
47. David Pimentel, "Energy and Land Constraints in Food Protein Production", *Science*, Nov. 21, 1975, pp. 754 ff.
48. Jean Meyer, cited by the U.S. Senate Select Committee on Nutrition and Human Needs, *Dietary Goals for the U.S.* (Washington, D.C., Feb. 1977), p. 44.
49. Arthur Simon, *Bread for the World*, (New York: Paulist Press, 1984 Revised Edition), p. 10.
50. Lappe, *Diet*, p. 92.

CHAPTER 5. *Judaism, Vegetarianism, and Ecology*

1. Shabbat 10a; Sanhedrin 7.
2. Ecclesiastes Rabbah 7:28.
3. Jerusalem Talmud, Kiddushin 4:12, 66d.
4. Baba Batra 2:8.
5. Baba Batra 2:8-9.
6. Baba Batra 158b.
7. Barachot 30:5
8. Story told by Rabbi Shlomo Riskin in "Biblical Ecology, A Jewish View," a television documentary, directed by Mitchell Chalek and Jonathan Rosen.
9. Sefer Ha-Chinuch 530.
10. Kiddushin 32a.
11. Baba Kamma 91b.
12. Berachot 52b.
13. Shabbat 67b.
14. Rabbi Samson Raphael Hirsch, *Horeb*, Dayan Dr. I. Grunfeld, trans. (London: Soncino Press, 1962), vol. 2, p. 282.
15. Ibid., p. 280.
16. Ecclesiastes Rabbah 1:18.
17. David Miller, *The Secret of Happiness* (New York: Rabbi David Miller Foundation, 1937), p. 9.
18. Lester R. Brown, *World without Borders* (New York: Vintage, 1972), pp. 95-96.
19. Frances M. Lappe, *Diet For a Small Planet*, (New York: Ballantine, 1984 revised edition), p. 9.
20. Ibid., p. 69.
21. "World Hunger Facts" (New York: American Friends Service Committee).
22. Lappe, *Diet*, p. 9.
23. Rabbi Adam D. Fisher, *To Deal Thy Bread To The Hungry*, (New York: Union of American Hebrew Congregations, 1975), p. 3.
24. Lappe, *Diet*, p. 76, based on presentation of agronomist Georg Borgstrom to the Annual meeting of the American Association for the Advancement of Science (AAAS), 1981.
25. "Facts of Vegetarian Society", Booklet of the North American Vegetarian Society (P.O. Box 72, Dolgeville, NY 13329), p. 3.

26. Lappe, *Diet*, p. 76, based on G. Borgstrom presentation.
27. Keith Akers, *A Vegetarian Sourcebook*, (New York: G. Putnam, 1983), p. 105.
28. "The Browning of America", *Newsweek*, Feb. 22, 1981, pp. 26 ff, cited in Lappe, *Diet*, p. 76.
29. John S. and Carol E. Steinhardt, "Energy Use in the U.S. Food System," *Science* (April 19, 1974).
30. Lappe, *Diet*, p. 10.
31. Ibid., p. 74, based on work of Drs. Marcia and David Pimentel at Cornell University.
32. Ibid.
33. Akers, *Vegetarian Sourcebook*, p. 87.
34. "Raw Material in the United States Economy 1900-1977", Technical Paper 47, U.S. Department of Commerce, U.S. Department. of Interior, Bureau of Mines, p. 3, cited by Lappe, *Diet*, p. 66.
35. Ibid., Table 2, p. 86.
36. Lester R. Brown and Gail W. Finsterbusch, *Man and His Environment: Food* (New York: Harper and Row, 1972), p. 69.
37. *Environmental Science and Technology*, Vol. 4, No. 12, 1970, p. 1098.
38. Ibid.
39. Georg Borgstrom, *The Food and People Dilemma* (Duxbury Press, 1973), p. 103, cited by Lappe, *Diet*, p. 84.
40. Akers, *Vegetarian Sourcebook*, pp. 87, 120-124.
41. Lappe, *Diet*, p. 80.
42. Ibid.
43. Ibid., p. 81.
44. Akers, *Vegetarian Sourcebook*, pp. 92, 120-124.
45. Lappe, *Diet*, p. 136.
46. Ron Litton, *Terracide* (Boston: Little, Brown, 1970) pp. 291-292.
47. Pamphlet of Rainforest Action Network, 300 Broadway, San Francisco, CA. 94133.
48. *Newsweek*, Sept. 14, 1987, p. 74.
49. Philip Pick, "The Sabbatical Year," *Tree of Life* (New York: Barnes, 1977), p. 64.

CHAPTER 6. *Judaism, Vegetarianism, and Peace*

1. Leviticus Rabbah 9:9.
2. Pirke Avot 1:12.
3. Yalkut Shimoni, Yithro 273.
4. Leviticus Rabbah 9:9.
5. Gittin 59b; the quotation is from Proverbs 3:17.
6. Genesis Rabbah 38:6.
7. Pirke Avot 5:11.
8. Rabbi Maurice Eisendrath, "Sanctions in Judaism for Peace," in *World Religions and World Peace*, Homer A. Jack, ed. (Boston: Beacon, 1968).
9. Rabbi J. David Bleich, "Vegetarianism and Judaism", Tradition, Vol. 23, No. 1 (Summer, 1987)
10. Nachmanides commentary on Deuteronomy 22:6.
11. Maimonides, Guide of the Perplexed, 3:17.
12. *Sefer Ha Chinuch*, Mitzvah 596.
13. Rabbi Elijah J. Schochet, *Animal Life in Jewish Tradition* (New York: Ktav, 1984), p. 217.
14. Rabbi Samson Raphael Hirsch, *Horeb*, Dayan Dr. I. Grunfeld, trans. (London: Soncino Press, 1962), Vol. 2, p. 328.
15. Ibid.
16. Quoted by Francine Klagsburn, *Voices of Wisdom* (New York: Pantheon Books, 1980), p. 458.
17. G. S. Arundale, "The World Crucifixion," *The Vegetarian Way, Proceedings of the 24th World Vegetarian Conference*, Madras, India (1977); 145.
18. Quoted by Barbara Parham, *Why Kill for Food*? (Denver, Colo.: Ananda Marga, 1979), p. 54.
19. Plato *Republic* 2. An historical review of the relationships among war, food production, and consumption is given by Dudley Giehl, *Vegetarianism: A Way of Life* (New York: Harper and Row, 1979), pp. 95-101.
20. Quoted in *The Vegetarian Way*, p. 12.
21. Mark Hatfield, "World Hunger," *World Vision* 19 (February 1975): 5.
22. *Staten Island Advance*, article by Susan Fogg, July 13, 1980, p. 1.
23. John S. and Carol E. Steinhart, "Energy Use in the U.S. Food

System," *Science* (April 19, 1974).

24. "How Vegetarians Can Help to End World Hunger," *Vegetarian Post*, Summer 1980.

25. David Pimenthal et al., "Energy and Land Constraints," *Science* (November 21, 1975): 757.

CHAPTER 7. *Questions and Answers*

1. Pesachim 109a.
2. Baba Batra 60b.
3. Ibid.
4. Rabbi J. David Bleich, "Vegetarianism and Judaism", Tradition, Vol. 23, No. 1 (Summer, 1987), p. 87.
5. Rabbi Alfred Cohen, "Vegetarianism from a Jewish Perspective", *Journal of Halacha and Contemporary Society*, Vol. I, No. II, (Fall 1981): 41,43.
6. Ibid., p. 43.
7. Rabbi Moshe Halevi Steinberg, "A Collection of *Responsa*" (questions and answers concerning conversion and converts), *Responsum #1*, p. 2.
8. Rabbi Abraham Isaac Kook, *A Vision of Vegetarianism and Peace*.
9. Shabbat 119; Sanhedrin 7.
10. Sanhedrin 59b.
11. Quoted by J. Green, "Chalutzim of the Messiah—The Religious Vegetarian Concept as Expounded by Rabbi Kook" (Lecture give in Johannesburg, South Africa, p. 2.)
12. Ibid.
13. Rabbi Samson Raphael Hirsch's commentary on Genesis 1:29.
14. Reverend A. Cohen, *The Teaching of Maimonides* (New York: Bloch Publishing Co., 1927), p. 178.
15. Ibid.
16. Ibid., pp. 178-79.
17. Ibid., p. 179.
18. Rabbi J. H. Hertz, *The Pentateuch and Haftorahs* (London: Soncino Press, 1958), p. 562.
19. Ibid.
20. Ibid., p. 559.
21. Rashi's commentary on Isaiah 43:23.

22. The Jewish Encyclopedia (1905), p. 628.
23. Rev. Dr. A. Cohen, *Soncino Chumash* (London: Soncino), p. 647.
24. Hertz, *Pentateuch and Haftorahs*, p. 562.
25. Ibid.
26. Berachot 17a.
27. Morris Laub, "Why the Fuss over Humane Slaughter Legislation?," Joint Advisory Committee Paper, January 26, 1966, p. 1. Also see the extended discussion in Rabbi E.J. Schochet's *Animal Life in Jewish Tradition* (New York: Ktav, 1985), pp. 283-287.
28. Ibid., p. 2.
29. Ibid.; Batya Bauman, "How Kosher Is Kosher Meat?," *The Reconstructionist* (April 17, 1970): 20-21.
30. Laub, "Why the Fuss?," Bauman, "How Kosher?," p. 21; Resolution of the Rabbinical Council of America, no. 16 (27th Annual National Convention, June 24-27, 1963).
30a. Quoted in *The Extended Circle*, edited by Jon Wynne-Tyson (Fontwell Sussex: Centaur Press, 1985), p. 28.
30b. Ibid, p. 16.
31. Cohen, "Vegetarianism...", p. 62.
32. Ibid.
33. *Josephus*, vol. 1 (Cambridge, Mass.: Loeb Classical Library, Harvard University Press, 1926), p. 7.
34. 2 Maccabees 5:27.
35. Cohen, "Vegetarianism...", p. 47.
36. Israel Zangwill, *Dreamer of the Ghetto*, 1898, p. 521.
37. Quoted in SANE (Committee for a Sane Nuclear Policy) slide show, "The Race Nobody Wins".
38. Cohen, "Vegetarianism...", p. 50.
39. Rabbi Zalman Schachter, foreward to Louis A. Berman's *Vegetarianism and the Jewish Tradition* (New York: Ktav, 1982), p. xv.
40. Maimonides, Mishneh Torah, Laws of Festivals, 6:18.
41. See "Involvement and Protest", Chapter 1 of *Judaism and Global Survival* by Richard H. Schwartz (New York: Atara, 1987).
42. Shabbat 54b.
43. Shabbat 55a.
44. Tanchuma to Mishpatim.
45. Ta'anit 11a.
46. *The Jewish Vegetarian*.

47. Diana K. Appelbaum, "Vegetarian Passover Seder," *Vegetarian Times 37* (April 1980): 44. Also, S. Strassfeld et al, *The Jewish Catalog*, p. 142.

48. Baba Batra 75a; Leviticus Rabbah 13:3; 22:10; Sanhedrin 99a.

49. *The Jewish Encyclopedia* (New York: Ktav), vol. 8, p. 38.

50. Ibid.

51. Ibid.

52. Rabbi J. David Bleich, "Vegetarianism and Judaism", Tradition, Vol. 23, No. 1 (Summer, 1987).

53. Ibid.

54. Steinberg, *Responsum* #1, p. 3.

55. Ibid.

56. J. Harris, "Killing for Food," in *Animals, Man, and Morals*, S. R. Godlovitch and John Harris, eds. (Gollancz, 1971), p. 109.

57. Nathaniel Altman, *Eating for Life* (Wheaton, Ill.:), Theosophical Pub. House, 1977), p. 6.

58. Fred Rosner, "Animal Experimentation: The Jewish View", in the 1986 *Jewish Directory and Almanac*, Ivan L. Tillem, ed. (New York: Pacific Press, 1986), p. 471.

59. Ibid.

60. Pamphlet of FARM (Farm Animal Reform Movement); P.O. Box 70123, Washington, D.C. 20088.

61. Ibid.

62. "Position Paper on the Vegetarian Approach to Eating", *Journal of the American Dietetic Association*, Vol. 77 (July 1980), p. 61.

63. Ibid., p. 62.

64. Ibid., p. 66.

65. For a complete discussion of natural hygiene, see Harvey and Marilyn Diamond, *Living Health* (New York: Warner Books, 1987).

66. Victor Sussman, *The Vegetarian Alternative* (Emmaus, Pa.: Rodale Press, 1978), p. 2.

67. Ibid.

68. For a more detailed discussion of why vegetarians do not eat fish, see Dudley Giehl, *Vegetarianism: A Way of Life* (New York: Harper and Row, 1979), pp. 59-70, and an editorial by Philip Pick, "Is Fish All Right?," *Jewish Vegetarian 48* (Spring 1979): 6-9.

69. Rabbi Samson Raphael Hirsch, *Horeb*, Dayan Dr. I. Grunfeld, trans. (London: Soncino Press, 1962), pp. 299-300.

70. Rabbi Moses Auerbach, "Smoking and the Halakhah", *Tradition*, 10 (3) (Spring, 1969), p. 50.

71. Ibid.

72. I am indebted to Ralph Meyer for this information related to Hitler's alleged vegetarianism, including copies of pages from several biographies which refer to Hitler's eating meat.

73. See, for example, John Toland's *Adolph Hitler* (Doubleday), p. 30, p. 54, p. 107, and p. 256) and Albert Speer's *Inside the Third Reich*, p. 89.

CHAPTER 8. *In The Camp of Kivrot Hata'avah*

1. Montagu made this assertion in an address to the 1973 Conference of the Humane Society, "Of Man, Animals, and Morals," delivered 19 Oct. 1973 in Atlanta. Also see his essay in *Animal Rights and Human Obligations*, ed. Regan and Singer.

2. Kenneth Clarke, "Animals and Men: Love, Admiration, and Outright War," in *Humans and Animals*, ed. John S. Baky (New York: H.W. Wilson, 1980).

3. Union Calendar #274: Human Food Safety and the Regulation of Animal Drugs: 27th Report of the Committee on Government Operations (U.S. Government Printing Office, 1985).

4. Orville Schell, *Modern Meat* (New York: Random House, 1984).

5. Louis Berman, *Vegetarianism and the Jewish Tradition* (New York: KTAV, 1982).

6. Louis I. Rabinowitz, "*Meat*," Encyclopedia Judaica, 11:1162.

7. This case is made by Peter Singer in his book *Animal Liberation: A New Ethics for Our Treatment of Animals* (Avon Books, 1975).

8. 255 Humphrey Street, Marblehead, MA 01945.

9. P.O. Box 1463, Baltimore, MD 21203.

CHAPTER 10. *Jewish Vegetarian Groups and Activites*

1. Joe Green, *The Jewish Vegetarian Tradition* (South Africa: 1969, p. 23.)

2. Philip Pick, "New Year Irresolution," editorial in *The Tree of Life*, Philip Pick, ed. (New York: A. S. Barnes, 1977), p. 20.

3. Based on the tradition of the Kabbalists, the first cup is white, the second white with some red added, the third roughly half and half, and the fourth mostly red with just a bit of white.

4. Arlene Groner, "The Greening of Kashrut—Is Vegetarianism the Ultimate Dietary Law?," *National Jewish Monthly* (April 1976): 12.

5. Nechemia Meyers, "120,000 vegetarians couldn't elect one Knesset deputy", *The Jewish Week*, Aug. 10, 1984.

6. Ibid; Joshua Brilliant, "Vegetarians to the front", *Jerusalem Port International Edition*, August 5-11, 1984.

7. *The Jewish Week*, Aug. 10, 1984.

8. Ibid; *Jewish Vegetarian* (June 1987): 14; *Jewish Vegetarian*, (Summer 1981): 19.

9. Information about *Amirim* was obtained from *Jewish Vegetarian* 46 (Autumn 1978): 13-15.

10. *Jewish Vegetarian* 38 (April 1976): 13.

11. Philip Pick, "The Source of Our Inspiration," *Jewish Vegetarian Society* Paper, p. 5.

12. *Jewish Vegetarian* 44 (Spring 1978): 43.

13. "Vegetarian Israel," *Jewish Vegetarian* 41 (April 1977): 28.

14. Ibid.

15. Ibid.

16. *Jewish Vegetarian*.

17. *Jewish Vegetarian*, (June 1987): 13.

18. *Jewish Vegetarian*, (Summer 1974): 24-25.

19. *Jewish Vegetarian*, (Summer 1981): 18.

20. Martha Meisels, "Vegetarian Paradise," *The Jerusalem Post International Edition*, Dec. 7, 1985, p. 17.

21. *The Jewish Vegetarian* (December 1986): 15, 16.

CHAPTER 11. *Biographies of Famous Jewish Vegetarians*

1. Information for this chapter was obtained from the *Encyclopedia Judaica* in addition to the sources noted.

2. S. Y. Agnon, *The Bridal Canopy*, pp. 222-23.

3. Philip Pick, "Agnon, Teller of Tales," in *The Tree of Life*, Philip Pick, ed. (New York: A. S. Barnes, 1977), p. 56.

4. Joe Green, "Chalutzim of the Messiah" (Lecture given in Johannesburg, South Africa, p. 1.)

5. *Jewish Vegetarian* 39 (August 1976): 22.
6. *Jewish Vegetarian.*
7. *Jewish Vegetarian* 29 (August 1973): 42.
8. *Jewish Vegetarian* 44 (Spring 1978): 19.
9. *Jewish Vegetarian* 40 (December 1976): cover.
10. Philip Pick, "The Source of Our Inspiration," a Jewish Vegetarian Society Paper, pp. 1-5.
11. *Jewish Vegetarian* 30 (Winter 1973): 17-19.
12. *Jewish Vegetarian* 33 (Autumn 1974): 27.
13. *Jewish Vegetarian* 40 (December 1976): 14-16.
14. *Jewish Vegetarian* 51 (Winter 1979): 10; further information was obtained from a letter sent by Rabbi Rosen to the author.
15. I. B. Singer, *The Estate*, New York: Farrar, Strauss, Giroux, 1969.
16. I. B. Singer, "The Slaughterer," short story in *The Seance and Other Stories*, New York: Farrar, Strauss, Giroux, 1968.
17. Jewish Vegetarian.
18. "When Keeping Kosher Isn't Kosher Enough," *New York Times*, September 14, 1977, p. 64.

CHAPTER 12. *Summary*

1. Rabbi Shlomo Riskin, "A Sabbath Week-Shabbat Ekev," *The Jewish Week*, Aug. 14, 1987, p. 21.

APPENDIX

1. Pirke Avot 2:21.
2. Shabbat 118b.
3. Conclusion of *Amidah*, prayer in sabbath morning services.
4. Sabbath morning prayer.
5. Samuel T. Coleridge, "The Ancient Mariner."
6. Rabbi A. J. Heschel, *The Insecurity of Freedom* (New York: Farrar, Strauss, and Giroux, 1967), p. 87.
7. Sota 14a.

Bibliography

Aleichem, Sholom. "Pity for Living Creatures." In *Some Laughter, Some Tears*, New York: G. P. Putnam's Sons, 1979.

The great Jewish writer tells how a young boy becomes aware of the concept of *tsa' ar ba' alei chayim* (prohibition of harming living creatures) through various incidents in his life.

Akers, Keith. *A Vegetarian Sourcebook*, Arlington, Virginia: Vegetarian Press, 1985.

Very comprehensive analysis of health, ecological, and ethical reasons for being vegetarian.

Altman, Nathaniel. *Eating for Life*. Wheaton, Ill.: Theosophical Publishing House, 1977.

An excellent, concise, but very complete, analysis of all aspects of vegetarianism.

Bargen, Richard (M.D.). *The Vegetarian's Self-Defense Manual*. Wheaton, Ill.: Theosophical Publishing House, 1979.

Thorough survey of professional literature related to vegetarian nutrition.

Barkas, Janet. *The Vegetable Passion*. New York: Scribner, 1975. Traces the history of vegetarianism from the biblical period to modern times.

Benjamin, Alice and Corrigan, Harriet. *Cooking with Conscience: A Book for People Concerned about World Hunger*. New York: Seabury, 1978.

Fifty-two healthful, simple meals based on vegetarian protein, eggs, and milk.

Berman, Louis. *Vegetarianism and Jewish Tradition.* New York: Ktav, 1981.

A comprehensive review of connections between Judaism and vegetarianism.

Brown, Lena. *Cook Book for Health* (Yiddish). New York: Jankovitz, 1931.

An early collection of Jewish vegetarian recipes.

Cohen, Noah J. *Tsa'ar Ba'alei Hayim—The Prevention of Cruelty to Animals, Its Bases, Development, and Legislation in Hebrew Literature.* New York: Feldheim, 1979.

An excellent and extremely comprehensive survey of the laws and lore relating to animals and their treatment in the Jewish tradition. A defense of *shechitah* (ritual slaughter).

David, Nathan S., ed. *The Voice of the Vegetarian* (Yiddish). New York: Walden Press, 1952.

A collection of essays devoted to ethical vegetarian ideals.

Diamond, Harvey and Marilyn Diamond. *Living Health* New York: Warner Books, 1987.

Dinshah, Freya. *The Vegan Kitchen.* Malaga, N.J.: American Vegan Society, 1987 (11th edition).

A wide variety of recipes that involve no animal products.

Dresner, Rabbi Samuel H. *The Jewish Dietary Laws, Their Meaning for Our Time.* New York: Burning Bush Press, 1959.

Fine discussion of the meaning of *kashrut.* States that the ideal Jewish diet is vegetarian and permission to eat meat was a concession. Discussion of compassion for animals in Jewish tradition and *shechitah* (ritual slaughter).

Ensminger, Ensminger, Konlande, Robson. *Food For Health, A Nutrition Encyclopedia.* California: Pegus Press, 648 West Sierra Ave., Clovis, CA 93612.

Ewald, Ellen Buchman. *Recipes for a Small Planet.* New York: Ballantine Books, 1973.

Many recipes for meatless meals. Complements *Diet for a Small Planet* by Frances Moore Lappe.

Fisher, Adam D. *To Deal Thy Bread to the Hungry.* New York: Union of American Hebrew Congregations, 1975.

Excellent review of the world hunger crisis and the Jewish tradition related to food and hunger. Suggest some steps to reduce malnutrition based on Jewish values.

Frankel, Aaron H. *Thou Shalt Not Kill or The Torah of Vegetarianism.* New York: 1896.

Freedman, Rabbi Seymour E. *The Book of Kashruth—A Treasury of Kosher Facts and Frauds.* New York: Block Publishing Co., 1970.

Much interesting material on *kashrut*. A very interesting chapter on fraud in meat supervision in hotels and catering halls.

Friedman, Rose. *Jewish Vegetarian Cooking*, New York: Thorsons, 1985.

The official cookbook of the International Jewish Vegetarian Society.

Gastwirth, Harold P. *Fraud, Corruption, and Holiness, The Controversy over the Supervision of the Jewish Dietary Practice in New York City,* 1881-1940. Port Washington, N.Y.: Kennikat Press, 1974.

An expose of unethical practices in *kashrut*, mostly related to meat and poultry supervision, in New York City, in the period from 1881 to 1940.

Giehl, Dudley. *Vegetarianism: A Way of Life.* New York: Harper and Row, 1979.

Excellent, thorough coverage of vegetarianism. Includes discussions of world hunger, animal rights, and ecological, economic, and religious factors. Foreword by Isaac Bashevis Singer.

Godlovitch, S., Godlovitch, R., and Harris, John, eds. *Animals, Men and Morals.* Gollancz, 1971.

An excellent collection of articles on the treatment of animals, including essays on factory farming and vegetarianism.

Green, Joe. *The Jewish Vegetarian Tradition.* South Africa: 1969.

Fine discussion of many aspects in the Jewish tradition, such as compassion for animals, that point toward vegetarianism as a Jewish ideal.

________. "Chalutzim of the Messiah—The Religious Vegetarian Concept as Expounded by Rabbi Kook" (lecture given in Johannesburg, South Africe).

Outline of some of Rabbi Kook's vegetarian teachings.

Groner, Arlene Pianko. "The Greening of Kashrut—Is Vegetarianism the Ultimate Dietary Law?" *The National Jewish Monthly* (April 1976).

Good summary of reasons why some Jews have become vegetarians.

Harrison, Ruth. *Animals Machines.* London: Vincent Street, Ltd., 1964.

Very detailed treatment of the tremendous cruelty involved in raising animals today. Shows that animals are treated like machines, not permitted any freedom or happiness.

Hirsch, Richard G. *Thy Most Precious Gift, Peace in the Jewish Tradition.* New York: Union of American Hebrew Congregations, 1974.

________. *The Way of the Upright, A Jewish View of Economic Justice.* New York: Union of American Hebrew Congregations, 1973.

Hur, Robin. *Food Reform: Our Desperate Need.* Austin, Tx.: Heidelberg, 1975.

Very well documented study showing the many values of a nutritionally balanced vegan diet based on plant foods.

Jewish Vegetarian, quarterly publication of the Jewish Vegetarian Society, London, England.

Katz, Rabbi Morris Casriel. *Deception and Fraud with a Kosher Front.* Endicott, N.Y.: Midstate Litho Inc., 1968.

Fraud and deception in kosher meat-packing plants.

Kalechofsky, Roberta. *Haggadah for the Liberated Lamb*, Marblehead, Mass.: Micah Press, 1984. The Passover message of liberation as a Seder supplement. Available in both English and English/Hebrew editions.

________. *The 6th Day of Creation*, Marblehead, Mass.: Micah Press, 1986.

Poems and short prose related to the treatment of animals.

________. "The Jewish Vegetarian Calendar", Marblehead, Mass.: Micah Press, 1987.

This unique calendar contains biblical quotations, poems, recipes, etc.

Kook, Rabbi Abraham Isaac. *A Vision of Vegetarianism and Peace* (Hebrew).

The vegetarian philosophy of this great Jewish leader and thinker. Rabbi Kook felt that God wanted people to be vegetarians but permitted meat as a concession, with many limitations, and that all creatures will be vegetarian in the messianic period, as they were in the Garden of Eden.

_______. "Fragments of Light: A View as to the Reasons for the Commandments," in *Abraham Isaac Kook*, a collection of Rabbi Kook's works, edited and translated by Ben Zion Bokser, New York: Paulist Press, 1978.

A summary of Rav Kook's thoughts on vegetarianism. Very powerful.

Lappe, Frances Moore. *Diet for a Small Planet*, New York: Ballantine Books, (Revised edition), 1982.

Convincingly shows the wastefulness of a meat-centered diet and that sufficient protein can be obtained from nonflesh foods.

Lappe, Frances Moore, and Joseph Collins. *Food First—Beyond the Myth of Scarcity*. Boston: Houghton Mifflin, 1977.

The real causes of widespread hunger and what can be done about it.

Leneman, Leah. *Slimming the Vegetarian Way*, England: Thorsons Publishers, 1980.

Nearly a hundred recipes to help people lose weight through a vegetarian diet.

Mason, Jim and Peter Singer. *Animal Factories*. New York: Crown, 1980.

"The mass production of animals for food and how it affects the lives of consumers, farmers, and the animals themselves."

Parham, Barbara. *What's Wrong with Eating Meat*? Denver, Colorado: Ananda Marga Publications, 1979.

Very concise and readable treatment of health, ecological, and political problems related to a meat-centered diet.

Pick, Philip, ed. *The Tree of Life, An Anthology of Articles Appearing in The Jewish Vegetarian*, 1966-1974. New York: A.S. Barnes, 1977.

A wide variety of essays on many aspects of the relationship between Judaism and vegetarianism. *Present Tense* magazine states, "Anyone who has ever felt queasy about any aspect of the meat business from the cruelty of slaughterhouses to the inefficiency of cattle as protein- sources will find much here that is thought-provoking and conscience-pricking."

Raisin, Jacob A. *Humanitarianism of the Laws of Israel—Kindness to Animals*. Jewish Tract #6, Cincinnati, Ohio: Union of American Hebrew Congregations.

Concise summary of laws in the Jewish tradition relating to kindness to animals.

Robertson, Laurel, et al. *The New Laurel's Kitchen: A Handbook for Vegetarian Cookery and Nutrition*. Berkeley, Calif.: Ten Speed Press, 1986.

Considered by many to be the best book on vegetarian nutrition. It has 512 pages, with nearly 200 pages on nutrition, including charts, tables, etc.

Rosen, Steven. *Food For the Spirit-Vegetarianism and the World Religions*, New York: Bala Books, 1986.
Shows connections between the major world religions and vegetarianism.

Rudd, G. L. *Why Kill for Food*? Madras, India: Indian Vegetarian Congress, 1956.
Very complete and well-written case for vegetarianism, from many points of view.

Scharfenberg, John A. *Problems with Meat.* Santa Barbara, Calif.: Woodbridge Press, 1979.
Report of scientific studies indicating several health hazards associated with eating meat. Many graphs, charts, and references.

Schell, Orville. *Modern Meat.* New York: Vintage Books, 1985.
Detailed discussion about problems related to the production of meat.

Schwartz, Richard. *Judaism and Global Survival*, New York: Atara Press, 1987.
Application of Jewish values to current critical issues such as hunger, pollution, resource scarcity, and the arms race.

Shoshan, A. *Man and Animal* (Hebrew). Jerusalem: Shoshanim, 1963.
A very thorough treatment of Jewish literature pertaining to the Jewish attitude toward animals from ancient to modern times.

Singer, Isaac Bashevis. "The Slaughterer," short story, translated by Mirra Ginsburg.
The Yiddish Nobel Prize winner tells of the great troubles that befall a Jew who becomes a slaughterer against his will.

Singer, Peter. *Animal Liberation.* New York: Avon Books, 1975.
Powerful argument for vegetarianism. Considers cruelty to animals from factory farming and scientific experimentation in great detail.

Spivack, Ellen Sue. *The Johnny Alfalfa Sprout Handbook.* 1986 P.O. Box 1751, Williamsport, PA 17703.

Author operates a world hunger charity and commercial sprouting business. Sprouts are an "instant" nutritious crop for hungry people. Comprehensive book covers both sprouting techniques and recipes.

Sussman, Victor. *The Vegetarian Alternative*. Emmaus, Pa.: Rodale Press, 1978.

Excellent, very complete, and well-documented case for vegetarianism, with many anecdotes.

Vegetarian Thought (Yiddish). Los Angeles, Calif.: 1929-30.

Vegetarian World (Yiddish). New York: 1921.

Wasserman, Debra and Charles Stahler. *No Cholesterol Passover Recipes.*

Contains 100 recipes without animal products, for beverages, salads, dressings, soups, side dishes, main courses, and desserts.

_______. *Vegetarianism for the Working Person..*

A wide variety of recipes for people with limited time.

"When Keeping Kosher Isn't Enough," *New York Times*, September 14, 1977, page 64.

A discussion of vegetarian attitudes and activities of American Jews.

Wynn-Tyson, Jon. *Food for a Future, The Ecological Priority of a Humane Diet*. London: Sphere Books Ltd., 1976.

A convincing case for the adoption of vegetarianism. Covers ecology, world hunger, health, cruelty to animals. Also has a good history of vegetarianism.

Subject Index